SHARKS AND LOACHES

braz walker

Distributed in the U.S.A. by T.F.H. Publications, Inc., 211 West Sylvania Avenue, P.O. Box 27, Neptune City, N.J. 07753; in England by T.F.H. (Gt. Britain) Ltd., 13 Nutley Lane, Reigate, Surrey; in Canada to the book store and library trade by Clarke, Irwin & Company, Clarwin House, 791 St. Clair Avenue West, Toronto 10, Ontario; in Canada to the pet trade by Rolf C. Hagen Ltd., 3225 Sartelon Street, Montreal 382, Quebec; in Southeast Asia by Y.W. Ong, 9 Lorong 36 Geylang, Singapore 14; in Australia and the south Pacific by Pet Imports Pty. Ltd., P.O. Box 149, Brookvale 2100, N.S.W., Australia. Published by T.F.H. Publications, Inc. Ltd., The British Crown Crown Colony of Hong Kong.

ISBN 0-87666-161-4

CONTENTS

4

INTRODUCTION

Somewhere beyond fishkeeping's first stages the aquarist encounters a number of fishes known popularly as "loaches" and others which are known as "sharks." The loaches are a more definable group, since the members all belong to the family Cobitidae, although there are members of some closely related families sometimes incorrectly called loaches. The "sharks," on the other hand, are freshwater aquarium fishes which belong to several families of carps and carp-like fishes, none of which is even remotely related to their giant cartilage-framed elasmobranch namesakes. The term has generally been applied as a trade name to certain fishes which seemed to have a rather shark-like appearance, usually beginning with a somewhat pointed front end and perhaps with a large dorsal fin similar to that of a shark and which is carried full-mast most of the time. There are even a few catfishes which are sometimes called "sharks."

Sharks and loaches, while not belonging to the same family, are nevertheless related. They all belong to the Superorder Ostariophysi, which includes carps and carp-like fishes, including loaches, catfishes, characins and South America's gymnotid eels or knife fishes. All ostariophysans possess a structure known as the Weberian apparatus which connects the gas bladder or swim bladder to the inner ear and, in some cases at least, makes the fish capable not only of receiving sound but generating it in an apparently coordinated manner.

With the exception of one or two catfishes which have been called "sharks," the other fishes discussed in this book all belong to the order Cypriniformes and the suborder Cyprinoidei. The catfishes belong to the order Siluriformes.

Most loaches and sharks have rather similar maintenance requirements which are not difficult to meet, although there are some noteworthy differences which will be taken into consideration elsewhere in the book. Among the loaches and sharks are some of the most spectacular freshwater fishes as well as some which are quite strange in appearance and almost unfishlike. Some have exceptional longevity for aquarium fishes and may live for quite a number of years.

Sharks and loaches, while admittedly an unscientific grouping, have a number of characteristic similarities which have caused many aquarists to form a mental grouping. Within their ranks are found fishes which are large and small, strange and beautiful, meek and aggressive and a hundred other facets between which comprise aquarium "personalities."

LOACHES

The loaches, as the members of the Old World family Cobitidae are known, range through Europe, Asia and parts of Africa. They reach their greatest diversity in the rain forests of southeastern Asia, although their forms and habits are quite various throughout their range.

Most loaches are not large in size and reach only a few inches in length, although some species of *Botia*, which is one of the more popular genera, are said to reach a length of about a foot in nature. Their body forms are quite varied. Some of the *Botia* species are quite chunky and heavy-bodied, while some of the popular "coolies" or *Acanthophthalmus* species are so worm-like that they hardly appear to be fishes as they wind their way over the aquarium floor. Still others such as *Cobitis* and *Misgurnus* have eel-like forms, as indicated in such names as *Misgurnus anguillicaudatus*. *Anguillicaudatus* means "eel-tail."

Many people confuse loaches with catfishes, although catfishes belong to an entirely different order. The two do, however, have external similarities which cause the confusion, and because of their look-alike nature they are still often classified together in aquarium show competition under the heading "Catfishes and Loaches," an entirely unwarranted combination which could be compared to lumping "Cats and Dogs" together for competition in a pet show. The confusion stems from the fact that both loaches and catfishes ordinarily have barbels or "whiskers" and that loaches often appear scaleless, just as do catfishes, which in most cases have naked skin. In reality, most

7

loaches have tiny scales, although they are often so reduced in size and so imbedded in the skin as to appear absent.

The barbels, as in the case of catfishes, are sensory organs of touch, taste and smell and are used to locate food items. Three or more pairs of barbels are present. The senses of taste and smell are highly developed in loaches and their ability to detect the presence of food in the aquarium is remarkable. For this reason and because of their eagerness to search out every scrap, a number of loaches, especially the worm-like or eel-like forms which have the ability to wiggle their way in, under and between almost every crack, crevice and object in the aquarium, are highly prized for their custodial performances.

The air bladder or gas bladder, which is ordinarily used by fishes as a hydrostatic organ in order to adjust their vertical position in the water with as little effort as necessary, is reduced in size, and since this makes most loaches heavier than water, they are for the most part bottom dwellers. The gas bladder is in two parts, with the front part enclosed in a bony capsule, and there is an opening on each side from which a duct leads to the skin above the pectoral fin. This places the external skin of the fish in linkage with the inner ear of the fish through the Weberian apparatus, the chain of modified vertebrae which was mentioned earlier as connecting the gas bladder with the inner ear. Because of this, certain loaches are extremely sensitive to changes in atmospheric pressure, reacting so nervously to rapid changes that they have actually been employed as "living barometers." Because of this peculiarity, many people call them "weather fish."

Aside from ordinary gill-breathing ability, some loaches are capable of supplementing their respiratory exchange through a system known as intestinal respiration. Actually what transpires is that air is taken from the atmosphere at the surface and "swallowed" into the intestinal tract. The intestinal tissue in these fishes is lined with numerous surface blood vessels and in some ways is similar to the vascular tissue found in our own lungs. Here the supplemental gas exchange is made, often allowing existence in waters which otherwise would be too polluted or too oxygen-poor for the fish to live. The used air, from which oxygen was exchanged for carbon dioxide, is simply expelled from the vent. While certain loaches regularly employ such surface respiration, in others it may be an indication of unacceptable aquarium conditions which if not corrected can lead to fish losses.

AQUARIUM FURNISHINGS

Most loaches are somewhat retiring, confining much of their activity to the twilight or dark. While they usually adjust rather quickly to aquarium living and lose their reluctance to feed in the daytime or with the light on, they show obvious discomfort unless there are adequate retiring facilities so that they can either appear or obscure themselves by choice. Preferred hiding places are under rocks, stumps or in caves or in any similar facility which might be present.

Aquarists who enjoy furnishing their aquariums with ceramic castles, stone pagodas and other decorations such as arched bridges will often find these artifacts occupied by loaches if they are present. Wormlike species (*Acanthophthalmus, Misgurnus*) seem to prefer hiding beneath objects of this type or similar pieces of material, while more free-swimming species such as *Botia* will often occupy the entrance or inside of such a piece of underwater architecture. Another favorite dwelling place is a halved coconut shell or half a vertically split flower pot. Enough of these hiding places should be provided to go around, specially for *Botia* and other large species, since they can be quite territorial and aggressive.

The "coolies" (*Acanthophthalmus* species) are a gregarious bunch which seem to prefer congregating under flattened objects such as flat rocks or underneath inside filters which rest on the bottom. Pieces of tree bark from heavy-barked hardwoods such as blackjack oak are especially appreciated. Upon occasion little coolies perhaps an inch in length suddenly appear in an aquarium where before there had only been a number of larger coolies.

Blackjack and other such bark can contain large amounts of tannic acid. While this can be beneficial and act as a natural form of supplement to the chemistry of the water, it is best to boil the bark before placing it in the aquarium or to soak it long enough to become thoroughly waterlogged and for some of the natural acid to leach out.

Some aquarists have even tried to simulate rain forest stream bottoms by using a well washed or boiled peat moss (or peat) as a covering for the aquarium floor. While this has shown promise in the development of a workable and dependable breeding procedure, for those who like to observe their fish regularly it is somewhat less than ideal since the fish spend most of their time hidden in the substrate.

WATER CONDITIONS

Most loaches do quite well under a wide range of water conditions. Since the tropical members of the family come most often from areas of high rainfall such as rain forests or rain forest-fed streams and lakes, it seems reasonable to assume that "normal" water conditions for the clan as a whole would be medium soft (5 DH or less) and with a pH of neutral to somewhat acid. In practice, however, they show a rather wide tolerance toward water variations and most seem to thrive in medium hard to soft water with a pH from as much as 7.6 downward to a fairly acid 6.4. Spawning, however, has been rare and mostly accidental for even those few species which finally have cooperated, and serious attempts would probably do well with slightly acid, rather soft water which might simulate more closely their native conditions. The Russians successfully spawn *Acanthophthalmus* using hormones.

Most loaches seem to prefer highly aerated water in spite of some possessing auxilliary breathing devices. Many species also prefer cooler water than many tropicals and show definite discomfort at more than 80° F. despite the heaviest aeration. Most tropical loaches seem to prefer the lower 70's to about 75° F., with some species such as those ranging into China and Japan and those from Europe (*Cobitis* and *Misgurnus*) easily tolerating much cooler water and thriving in the unheated aquarium.

While "old" water such as that advocated a few years ago by some of the world's leading aquarists will be tolerated, as with most fishes at least an occasional partial change of water is much appreciated, and its worth will be obvious in the increased activity and vitality of the fish. Removal and replacement of 25% of the water every two or three weeks seems to "pep" the fish up considerably.

Some species, such as *Acanthophthalmus* species, the so-called "coolies," show rather low levels of tolerance for polluted water caused by overfeeding or overpopulation. For this reason they are very useful "barometers" for aquarium conditions, showing distress very plainly when the sand or water becomes foul, although the water may remain clear. When a number of coolies in the same aquarium begin to display a great deal of nervous activity, swimming rapidly all over the tank and up and down the sides, it is wise to check the sand, especially under rocks and other solid objects, to be sure there is no decaying organic matter. Dirty filters can be another source of pollution.

The apparent "reversal" in aquarium water theory is less difficult to explain or understand than one might imagine. In Europe especially, the classic approach to aquarium keeping has placed as much emphasis on the horticultural aspect of the hobby as the fishkeeping end. Luxuriant plant growths plus a relative sparseness of fishes produced a situation which actually at times came amazingly close to the theoretical "balanced aquarium" in which fish would produce the nutrition required by the plants with waste products and carbon dioxide, while the plants would in turn produce oxygen and even food for the fish. Occasional "topping up" with rainwater or distilled water, plus feeding mostly with natural or living foods, resulted in a reasonably reciprocal situation, even without what we think of as minimal aeration and filtration.

Today's fast filtration systems allow heavier feeding and greater populations, and even when clear water is maintained there is a buildup of chemical waste and urine which can become quite "thick." This is avoided by regular partial water changes.

FEEDING LOACHES

Most loaches present few problems as far as feeding is concerned. In nature they seem primarily to feed on various forms of larval insects plus worms, crustaceans and algae or other vegetation. Some species are more specialized in their fare than others, and this will be noted under separate species listings in cases where various requirements are significant.

Loaches are primarily bottom feeders, rooting along the aquarium floor in search of the small aquatic life upon which they feed in nature or whatever substitute the aquarium keeper might offer them. Because of this they should be given food which sinks in enough quantity to fully provide for them. At the same time, it is best never to satiate them, since leaving a bit of an edge on their appetites will cause them to search out scraps left by others, helping to avoid pollution from overfeeding.

Brine shrimp, either live or frozen, ground beef heart, tablet or pellet food and sunken flake food are relished by most. Chopped earthworms or whole ones for those able to swallow them, as well as white worms (enchytrae) or tubifex, are particularly appreciated. For the partial vegetarians, cooked oatmeal or rolled oats is excellent and highly nutritious, as well as alfalfa rabbit food pellets or cooked spinach. Some larger species of *Botia* are very fond of red ramshorn snails, which they either deftly "jerk" from their shells or can sometimes even be heard "crunching" on, as snails which are small enough are crushed in their pharyngeal teeth ; like other Cypriniformes they have no teeth in the jaws. Other snails seem of less interest to them, although mystery snails are sometimes molested and even killed by large *Botia*.

BREEDING CONDITIONS

Among the tropical loaches, there have been occasional breedings of a few species in the aquarium, but the information resulting from the spawnings is hardly sufficient to give flawless descriptions. There have been several reports of *Acanthophthalmus* and at least one species of *Botia* spawning, and not only have there been several quite different descriptions of the procedures, but there have been several NON-descriptions, babies or half-grown adults appearing in a tank where only full-grown fish had been before.

Since spawning of coolies, probably *Acanthophthalmus semicinctus*, has been reported most often, it is more feasible to work out a "pattern" for their spawning behavior and the circumstances which seem to lead to it. Combining the collectable information, I have tried to work out a reasonable approach.

The breeding aquarium should be at least 10 gallons. It should be filled with soft water, preferably 2 DH or less. This is based on two things: in southeastern Asia where they are found the water is almost invariably among the softest water found in nature, and I have never heard of a spawning or a hatching which took place in other than a soft water aquarium. While pH may be a bit less important, since tolerance for a considerable spread has been reported, 7.0 or less seems reasonable, because natural waters of their native areas are usually acid.

Coolies like cover. Aside from providing caves, flat rocks and pieces of wood under which they can congregate, a condition which has been present during several spawnings has been a heavy layer of plant detritus and other "mulm" covering the bottom. Better yet is a layer of well washed peat moss, for which unfortunately they will show their appreciation by remaining hidden in it completely out of sight. Col. Jorgen Scheel, world renowned killifish expert, is an avid proponent of the use of peat in the aquarium as a water conditioner which is without match. He also feels it gets better as it goes along, producing enzymes and other beneficial substances which have remarkable influence on the physical well-being of certain aquarium fishes including *Acanthophthalmus*, which spawned for him in aquaria with peat covering the bottom.

Others have also had spawning occur with such a floor covering, and there is little doubt that this simulates natural conditions since there is often a layer of decaying vegetation covering the bottom of streams and swamps where they live.

While eggs have been found under bottom filters, rocks and other objects, most reports in which any preliminary indication that the coolies had family plans describe a

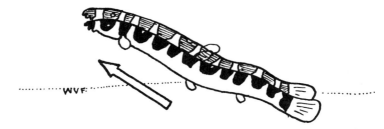

From von Filek.

The spawning behavior of *Acanthophthalmus semicinctus* is probably typical of that of all elongate loaches, involving a parallel swim toward the surface and the male coiling around the female. Few spawning rituals have been watched from start to finish because the abundance of bottom cover generally needed for spawning interferes with viewing. Drawings based on those of W. von Filek.

15

definite pattern of courtship. The unmistakable part of the courtship pattern is "parallel swimming," the male and female seeming almost to be attached by some invisible thread so that their bodies seem to move in unison as they swim rapidly or even dash around the aquarium, up and down the glass, behind rocks, etc. Previous to this there is usually chasing, male pursuing female determinedly. Fondling of the female by the male may or may not be a part of courtship, apparently depending on circumstances, although the case may simply be that it often goes unnoticed. "Fondling" consists of the male gently searching over the female with his barbels, especially in the pectoral region, sometimes embracing her by bending the forward part of his body over hers or bending his tail over her body.

When parallel swimming finally occurs, spawning is not far away. The pair rises as if locked together, with bodies gently quivering, and often as they near the surface the eggs are released and fertilized, usually about forty at a time. This is repeated until the female is exhausted of eggs.

Some observers have felt that the fish were somehow actually fastened together physically either with the pectoral fins or perhaps the preorbital spine. This is not confirmed, although their movements are amazingly sympathetic and coordinated. Careful observation of future spawnings will clarify this.

SPECIES OF LOACHES

As far as the aquarist is concerned most of the loaches encountered thus far have belonged to seven genera; *Acanthophthalmus, Acanthopsis, Botia, Cobitis, Lepidocephalus, Misgurnus* and *Noemacheilus*. All, with the exception of *Noemacheilus*, which is the largest genus of loaches, possess a spine beneath the eye which in most cases is erectile and can be locked in place as a defense mechanism. In *Misgurnus* the spine is beneath thick skin and is less obvious than in others.

genus *Acanthophthalmus*

The genus *Acanthophthalmus* contains the elongated, worm-like and often quite colorful little fishes which are collectively known as "coolies" or "coolie loaches." This is actually a degeneration of the specific name of one of the first species to be imported, *A. kuhlii*. Through common usage and the fact that people seem to have found some mental affinity between "coolie" and these little loaches which have often been employed in a custodial or janitorial capacity because of their willingness to search out scraps, the name stuck.

Coolies have no scales on their heads and their eyes are covered with transparent skin. There are usually three or four pairs of little barbels which give them a rather quaint appearance, and there is no lateral line. The dorsal fin is located well posterior to the insertion of the ventral or pelvic fins. Many of the coolies are colorfully banded in distinctive patterns which have been used as the basis for separating into a number of species. Since there are numerous pattern variations, especially in *A. semicinctus* which may range from almost total lack of dark patterning to an almost totally dark fish, with various degrees of banding between, at least some of the described species are doubtful. Often these color varieties are caught together, and few shipments come in which do not contain several "different" kinds of coolies.

As far as the aquarist is concerned the two most important *Acanthophthalmus* species are *A. kuhlii* and *A. semicinctus*, known respectively in the trade as the "giant coolie" and the "regular coolie" or perhaps just "coolie." Others are occasionally brought in and these are also covered in the species descriptions.

ACANTHOPHTHALMUS JAVANICUS Bleeker, 1860
Java loach

From Java and Sumatra (also recorded by Hugh M. Smith from Thailand) comes this unbanded species of coolie, *Acanthophthalmus javanicus*. Body and head are uniform reddish brown, lighter below, with a single black bar at the base of the caudal. There are several other species of unbanded coolies also, such as *A. borneensis* Boulenger, *A. pahangensis* Beaufort and *A. pangia* Hamilton, but these are of less interest to the aquarist than the more handsome banded members of the clan.

This is a typical peaceful and undemanding *Acanthophthalmus* species. Care and conditions as for others of the genus.

Reaches a length of about 3-3½ inches or slightly over 8 cm.

ACANTHOPHTHALMUS KUHLII (Cuvier, 1846)
Kuhli loach; Giant coolie

The true *Acanthophthalmus kuhlii* is the fish from which the common name "coolie loach" originated, although the name is applied to all the banded members of the genus including *A. semicinctus*, most often imported of the genus, and other more heavy-bodied and larger members such as *A. myersi*. Ranging rather widely from Java, Sumatra, Borneo, Malaya and Thailand into Burma and India, this is a variable species as far as pattern is concerned.

In his book *The Freshwater Fishes of Siam, or Thailand*, Hugh M. Smith described *A. kuhlii* as having 12 to 15 alternating cross-bands of red and black, and with the

This *Acanthophthalmus*, like most specimens seen in dealers' tanks, presents identification problems. It seems to agree with the fish known as *A. kuhlii sumatranus* in the small number of short, partially divided bands. Whether this name represents anything more than just a color pattern of *A. kuhlii* is doubtful. Photo by G.J.M. Timmerman.

end of the dorsal over or slightly in advance of the anal fin. These broad transverse bands of black and red have earned for the fish the vernacular name *pla prong oy* or "sugarcane-joint fish" in allusion to the definitely "jointed" appearance of its elongated form. It is a bit larger and more heavily-bodied than *A. semicinctus*.

While a number of species and subspecies of coolies have been described on a basis of pattern variations, nomenclature and validity are uncertain. Some are undoubtedly allied to this species.

This is a beautiful and peaceful species which reaches a length of a little over 3 inches. Its quaintness and odd appearance combined with its handsome pattern make it immediately appealing. Despite its definite preference for low-light situations, like other coolie species it soon starts to come out at feeding time. The search continues after the lights are out, performing very useful custodial services by gleaning uneaten scraps which might be missed by fishes with less body dexterity. Small live and frozen foods, top quality pellet and tablet foods and other foods reaching the bottom should be provided, not relying solely on the scavenging ability of the fish to survive.

Water should be clean and well aerated. Medium soft water with pH around neutral to slightly acid seems preferable, although the range of tolerance is rather wide. Temperatures in the mid-70's keep the fish comfortable.

ACANTHOPHTHALMUS MYERSI Harry, 1949
Myers loach; Slimy Myersi

Acanthophthalmus myersi is similar in many ways to *A. kuhlii* and is one of the larger and heavier-bodied species which are sold as "giant coolies." It is found in southeastern Thailand on Kao Sabap. There are usually 10-14 broad black or dark brown bands which are quite wide and seem often to completely encircle the fish, even connecting on the belly in some specimens, while in most spe-'

The loach commonly called *Acanthophthalmus myersi*. Notice that the bands are large, not divided, and extend well beyond the middle of the sides. This fish shows a great deal of variation from almost solid black to heavily spotted or mottled . Photo by M. Chvojka.

cies the belly is pale. These bands are not paired and they are uniform in color. Light interspaces are yellow to salmon red.

Myers' loach is certainly one of the more handsome coolies. Like others, it is easily cared for but is a retiring creature which prefers to hide under rocks, in caves or coconut shells or under pieces of waterlogged driftwood or hardwood bark. Some aquarists provide coolie species with a bottom covering of peat moss. This simulates the natural mulm often found on the bottoms of forest streams where the fish are found and, while it is quite willingly accepted by the loaches, it is of some less benefit to the aquarist who likes seeing his fish more than just occasionally.

All kinds of small live food are eagerly searched out, but like other coolies, any meat or fish-based food is eaten with gusto. Pellet and tablet foods are excellent as a staple. Freeze-dried tubifex are a favorite when fed in one of the little plastic feeding bells designed to hold them near the bottom so that the loaches can find them. This is one of the best and most easily handled of non-living foods for almost the entire cobitid or loach family.

A. myersi reaches a length of a bit over 3 inches or about 8 cm. Some authors consider this a subspecies of *A. kuhlii*. This fish is being regularly spawned in Russia through the use of hormones as a spawning stimulant.

ACANTHOPHTHALMUS ROBIGINOSUS Raut 1957

This west Javanese loach is described by Sterba as being muddy yellow-brown to bright rust-red on the body with the belly paler but never white. There are about 21 narrow dark brown transverse bands which reach to below the middle of the side. The bands have no pale inner zones as in some species, and there is a steel blue luster to the sides by reflected light.

Spawning is not described, although in males all the fins are larger and the second pectoral ray is thickened.

This is one of the smaller species, reaching about 2-2½ inches or 5-6 cm. Care and feeding as for other similar species.

ACANTHOPHTHALMUS SEMICINCTUS
Fraser-Brunner, 1940
Half-banded coolie loach

This is the common "coolie" of the aquarium, since it is most frequently imported from the East Indies where it is found. There is considerable variation in pattern in this fish, and many authorities feel that some of the "species" which have been described on a basis of color pattern are simply variations of *A. semicinctus*. There are reports that these are at times caught together in the same net and seem not to be separable on any basis but color. This would rule out their being subspecies, since a subspecies must be a geographically definable population which differs in taxonomy from the species. Their ranges must not overlap. Species, on the other hand, are defined as interbreeding natural populations which are reproductively isolated from other groups. Since these fish apparently live and breed communally, it is questionable whether more than one species can be legitimately defined.

In *A. semicinctus* the bands all cross the back and end about midside. They usually number 12-16 excluding the three on the head and the one on the caudal base. The bars are quite variable in form, sometimes being connected at the bases in pairs so that saddle-shaped wedges are formed which may have yellowish or pinkish centers. In

Acanthophthalmus, probably *robiginosus*. This species, whatever name it should properly bear, is easily identified by the narrow dark bands and wide light interspaces. It is not commonly seen. Photo by Dr. Herbert R. Axelrod.

other specimens there may be several bars connected to form a solid block in one place or another. The belly is usually pinkish-white to salmon. The anal is inserted just at the posterior end of the dorsal, and the ventrals are located about midway on the underside. The second pectoral ray is thickened in mature males and all fins are said to be smaller in females.

An interesting pair of *Acanthophthalmus semicinctus*. The specimen on top is probably somewhat albinistic, but the dark eye shows it is not a true albino. The short bands, not reaching much or at all below the middle of the sides, and their irregular appearance are characteristic of this species. Photo by R. Zukal.

Care is as for other species of *Acanthophthalmus*. This is almost invariably a favorite of those who keep it. Length of up to 3¼ inches or 8 cm.

Two other species of banded *Acanthophthalmus* are described from North Borneo. *A. lorentzi* is described as having six or seven bands on the body, rather thin lips and no oblique stripe before the eye. *A. sandakanensis* has four or five cross bands on the body, thicker lips and an oblique stripe before the eye.

ACANTHOPHTHALMUS SHELFORDI Popta, 1901
Shelford's loach

There are several species of *Acanthophthalmus* or "coolie" loaches which are native to Borneo, some of which are banded and others which are not. One of the banded species having a quite handsome and distinctive pattern is Shelford's loach, *Acanthophthalmus shelfordi*, which has occasionally been imported to Europe and America.

Like other coolies, this is a long-bodied, worm-like little fish whose lead-bottomed swimming efforts confine it mostly to the aquarium floor. Like other *Acanthophthalmus* spp. however, it can, when occasion demands, swim at breakneck speed through the water, up, down and around every obstruction in the aquarium, testing the patience of even the most skilled net-handler with its serpentine swimming actions. Like an airplane, as soon as the coolie shuts its motor off, it sinks back to the ground.

In *A. shelfordi* there is a dark band several times wider than the eye just across the nape, and on the body there are two rows of dark bands, the lower row not reaching the middle of the dorsal surface. Between these alternating rows there are sometimes delicate narrow pink stripes, although there is considerable variation and at times the lower row of bars or even both may be reduced to alternating or irregular blotches.

25

genus *Acanthopsis*

The loaches of this genus have very long and slender bodies with the head and snout also unusually long and compressed. The odd appearance resulted in the name "horse-face loach" becoming popular. There is a small bifid or two-pronged spine which can be erected and locked in place for defense located suborbitally, and there are eight barbels.

Interesting, unusual and non-aggressive fishes.

ACANTHOPSIS CHOIRORHYNCHUS (Bleeker, 1854)
Horseface loach

The "horseface loach" is common through southeastern Asia, Sumatra, Borneo, and India. It is found not only in clear, swift-running hill streams with sand or gravel bottoms but also in turbid swamp streams with mud bottoms. While there are a number of color variations throughout the range, the basic color is pale yellowish or ocher, which lightens to whitish toward the belly. This may be adorned by a series of short vertical bars, a row of dots or blotches, a single dark longitudinal band, or nothing. The fins are yellowish or colorless, sometimes with brownish bars or dots on the dorsal and caudal.

The color and pattern of the fish give them a remarkable camouflage, and in nature it has been observed that the only indication of their presence as they moved across the sandy bottom of a clear stream was their shadows. As if the ability to blend almost perfectly with their background is not enough, when the horseface loach is frightened it simply dives into the sand, a defense mechanism shared also by certain other loaches and other fishes. These fish are well designed for sand-diving, which can be better understood after attempting to remove one or more from a well-planted aquarium with a fine sand bottom.

This is strictly a bottom-dweller which feeds in nature

on nematodes (worms) and other small aquatic animals such as insect larvae and diatoms. In the aquarium small worms, live or frozen brine shrimp and bloodworms or similar larvae are eagerly accepted. Finely ground beef heart or ox heart will also usually be eaten.

Although this rather comical-looking fish reaches eight inches or more in nature, half this in the aquarium is a large size. It is an inoffensive fish which does well in a community aquarium of fishes its size.

Acanthopsis choirorhynchus has not spawned in the aquarium to date as far as is known. Sexes are easily distinguished since the pectoral fins of the male are much larger than those of the female.

This fish has also been sold in America as the "Mr. Clean eel."

The horseface loach is commonly displayed on light sand bottoms and assumes such a light grayish-white color that it is hard to spot in the tank. The elongate snout or face is very distinctive among the loaches seen in captivity. Photo by R. Zukal.

genus *Botia*

The genus *Botia* contains a number of striking species, one of which, *B. macracantha*, is among the most beautiful of freshwater fishes. All species are equipped with a bifid or two-pronged suborbital spine which can be erected and locked in place as a defense mechanism. Both fishes and snakes have been found which have swallowed *Botia*, only to have the spines erected and pierce their own throats, obviously to the predator's demise.

BOTIA BERDMOREI (Blyth, 1860)
Berdmore's loach

Berdmore's loach, ranging from Burma to Thailand, is considered by H.M. Smith to probably be a geographic variation or other normal variation of *Botia hymenophysa*, which is a very variable species. Its importance to the aquarium is because of its quite different appearance in comparison to the tiger loach. Day noted earlier the great similarity between *B. berdmorei* and *B. hymenophysa*, citing the differences as being in the dorsal fin, with 13-15 branched rays for *B. berdmorei* and 11-13 for *B. hymenophysa*, plus differences in color. The dorsal fin of *B. berdmorei* is inserted well behind the ventrals, while in *B. hymenophysa* the dorsal is in advance of the ventrals.

Botia berdmorei is cream to buff or delicate ocher with 10 or 11 darker vertical bands from the dorsal side to the abdomen. Two black bands extend from behind the eyes, continuing on the sides as rows of blotches. There is a dark band from the eye to the snout, and the rostral barbels are black. The dorsal fin has three or four bands or rows of spots and is rather yellowish. The caudal base has two or three bands.

Other considerations are the same as for *Botia hymenophysa*.

28

BOTIA BEAUFORTI Smith, 1931
Beaufort's loach

Botia beauforti from Thailand is one of the less "flat-bottomed" of the *Botia* species, the underside being a bit convex in profile just as the upper and giving a more cylindrical impression. The body and sides are a light grayish green and there are four rows of dark brown dots or spots running longitudinally on the body. Each spot is surrounded by a pale ring. From the head almost to the end of the dorsal are five dark brown lines followed by dots, and on

Botia beauforti is not commonly seen in the aquarium and is often misidentified as the common and variable *Botia hymenophysa*. The elongate spots in front of the dorsal fin are usually distinctive, but there is also an easy difference in the fins: *Botia hymenophysa* has about twelve rays in the dorsal (count at the base of the fin) while *Botia beauforti* has only nine. Photo by H. Hansen, Aquarium Berlin.

the head are several curved stripes. The dorsal and caudal are bright orange with rows of darker spots, the anal is yellow and the pectorals and ventrals are light orange. This is one of the most beautiful *Botia* species.

B. beauforti reaches a length of 20-25 cm. (8-10 inches) in Thailand and like some of its relatives is known by the local name *pla mu* or hog fish because of its "tusks." It is closely related to *B. berdmorei*, which is a rather variable species in pattern and color, leaving this possibility open also for *B. beauforti* to come in a range of models.

Individuals may become aggressive toward other fishes, although they do much better in groups or schools, which is also their preference in nature. Hiding places and "elbow room" should be plentiful. A large aquarium is recommended.

BOTIA HORAE Smith, 1931
Skunk loach

This Thai loach is one of the smaller *Botia* species, not often reaching more than 2½ inches in the aquarium. Although it is often described as completely peaceful, *Botia horae* despite its size can be quite aggressive, especially to its own kind, unless plenty of hiding places are available.

The body coloration of this handsome little fish is basically light brown or tan. A broad black stripe extends from the tip of the snout along the dorsal surface to the root of the tail, and there is a broad black band across each side of the caudal peduncle or the base of the tail. The forked caudal (tail) fin is yellowish with rows of brownish dots, and there are four vertical bars rather evenly spaced on the sides, although these are sometimes obscure. At times there are hints of metallic blue or green on some of the darker areas when viewed in reflected light.

No reports have been made of breeding.

A long-lived, durable and undemanding little fish.

BOTIA HYMENOPHYSA (Bleeker, 1852)
Tiger loach; Tiger botia

The tiger loach, *Botia hymenophysa*, is one of the larger species of *Botia*, attaining a reported length of up to 12 inches in nature. Although in the aquarium a fish half this length can be considered exceptionally large, at that size there are few aquarium fishes with which it cannot effectively compete, even large and pugnacious cichlids. Widespread in Thailand, Greater Sunda Islands and Malaya.

This is one of the more elongate, less compressed *Botia* species, the body of a plump, maturing specimen being almost cylindrical. The fish is rather retiring at first, especially in a small or medium aquarium, and should be fur-

Botia hymenophysa has so many color patterns that it is difficult to say which is the most common. The barred pattern shown here can vary widely in the width of the dark bars. Photo by G.J.M. Timmerman.

The pale phase of *Botia hymenophysa* has indistinct bars and prominent spots, resembling *Botia beauforti*. Notice that the dorsal fin is long, with about twelve rays in this species, a count easily made in the aquarium. Photo by G. Marcuse.

nished with hiding or retiring places such as rocky caves. Although somewhat nocturnal by nature, in a very large and roomy aquarium a strange personality change comes over the fish in some instances and it becomes more than just a casual namesake for its feline counterpart. Lacking fear, if not respect, of even larger fishes than itself, a tiger loach will often select a particular fish which is an irritation to it, and this fish will be methodically harassed at every opportunity for a rear approach until the victim finally turns on the aggressor and reverses the situation. If "the worm never turns," the molesting may become so serious as to necessitate removal of either the aggressor or the recipient.

Acanthophthalmus javanicus. Photo by Dr. Herbert R. Axelrod.

Acanthophthalmus kuhlii. Photo by A. Van den Nieuwenhuizen.

Coloration consists primarily of a gray-brown body encircled by a series of vertical bands which are darker. There are slight color variations among individuals of *Botia hymenophysa* which may be attributable at least in part to differences in age. Since this is a widespread species, this could also be due to territorial or population differences.

Botias are not always easy to identify. This rather non-descript specimen has twelve dorsal rays, no spots before the dorsal fin, and the general shape of *Botia hymenophysa*. It should be mentioned, however, that there are several other Indian and Southeast Asian botias which are seldom seen by aquarists, making identifications even more uncertain. Photo by H. Hansen, Aquarium Berlin.

Although there are times when the bands appear simply to be darker than the interspaces, in reflected lighting the entire pattern takes on a rather striking bluish or greenish luminescence. Fins are ordinarily translucent yellow which at times can take on a faint blush of red or orange, especially in mature fish.

As in the case of *Botia modesta* and other large *Botia* species, the armament system is alluded to by the natives throughout Thailand in calling the fish *pla mu* or "hog fish" or *pla mu kang lai*, meaning "striped hog fish." Actually, the tiger loach wields these "tusks" quite deftly in combat just as in the case of its namesake, so the allusion is a good one.

This is also one of the *Botia* species which is an effective snail eradicator. For those plagued by overpopulation of ramshorn snails, the larger *Botia* including this species can be introduced as a very practical solution to their control. The snails are excellent food for the loaches, and if you find the snail population being devastated beyond your wishes, removal of the loaches temporarily or permanently usually results in reestablishment of the mollusk population.

BOTIA LECONTEI Fowler, 1937

Botia lecontei is quite similar to *Botia modesta* in appearance except that the body is proportionately longer and more slender in *B. lecontei* and the dorsal originates over the base of the ventrals and midway between the tip of the snout and the caudal base. In *B. modesta* the dorsal origin is in advance of the ventrals and closer to the snout than the caudal base.

Body greenish to blue-grey, pale on underside. There is a black, round blotch on the caudal root which is more or less distinct according to conditions and individual specimens. Fins are yellowish to reddish.

Care is as for other *Botia* species.

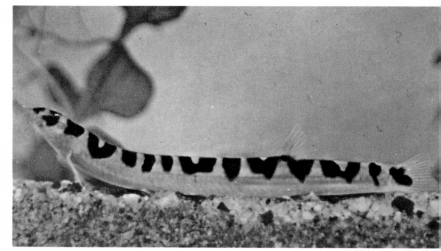

Acanthophthalmus semicinctus. Photo by Dr. Herbert R. Axelrod.

Another color variety of *Acanthophthalmus semicinctus*. Photo by Dr. Herbert R. Axelrod.

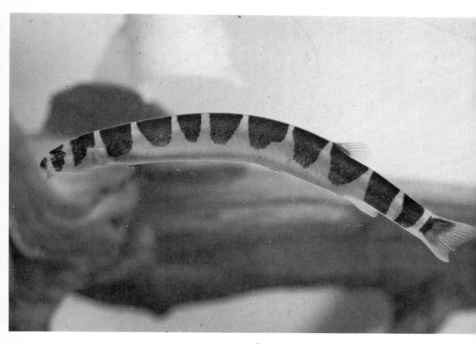

Typically patterned *Acanthophthalmus myersi*. Photo by Dr. Herbert R. Axelrod.

BOTIA LOHACHATA Chaudhuri, 1912
Reticulated loach

The reticulated loach is one of the several more slender and elongated *Botia* species with a barred patterning over the body and with bars and other markings on the dorsal and caudal fins. The body color is basically a silvery yellow or silvery gray, with darker vertical bars which branch or fork into a rather y-shaped pattern near the dorsal surface. There are several color and pattern variations which are apparently geographic. *Botia lohachata* is native to East Pakistan where it is said to inhabit standing

The relatively rare *Botia lecontei* supposedly differs from the more common *Botia modesta* in having a slimmer body, the dorsal fin placed directly over the ventral fins, and a more distinct spot at the base of the tail. The shape and color vary with feeding and the general condition of the fish, and the fin placement is often hard to decide one way or the other. Photo by M. Chvojka.

The reticulated loach commonly deserves its name, but not in every pattern. In the individual shown here the bands on the sides are nearly straight and unbroken. Photo by H. Hansen.

An almost solid black *Acanthophthalmus myersi* found in the same
shipment as the normally colored specimen shown with it. Photos
by V. Elek.

A bizarrely patterned coolie loach. This is probably just a very dark and badly patterned *Acanthophthalmus myersi*. Photo by Dr. Herbert R. Axelrod.

Acanthophthalmus semicinctus. Photo by Dr. Herbert R. Axelrod.

and flowing waters down to the smallest puddles. A similar fish, which may be this species or a subspecies, is found in India. It is reportedly smaller and less colorful.

Like other *Botia* species, it possesses a bifid or two-pronged suborbital or under-eye spine which can be erected and locked in place as a defense mechanism.

Reaching a length of about 4 inches, the reticulated loach seems to prefer warmer water than most, being comfortable at 77-82° F., although lower temperatures are easily tolerated. The water should be clear and well aerated. This is a retiring species, but will learn to come out at feeding time, even taking dried food from the surface. Live foods, especially tubifex and other worms, are preferred but the species is omnivorous. Unless algae is growing in the aquarium, occasional vegetation should be offered.

An example of the individual differences often seen in *Botia loha-chata*. These two fish are probably from the same place. Notice that the dark bands in the fins are few and wide. Photo by M. Chvojka.

Compared to the fish shown earlier, this might almost be a different species. However, it is just an extremely reticulated *Botia lohachata* in what is considered to be the most common pattern. A broad range of individual color variations connects this fish with the straight-banded one on an earlier page. Photo by H. Hansen, Aquarium Berlin.

BOTIA LUCASBAHI Fowler, 1937
Barred loach

Botia lucasbahi is quite similar in appearance to *Botia hymenophysa*, the tiger loach or tiger botia. This is a smaller and more colorful fish than the tiger, however, and lacks the often malevolent disposition of the other.

This three-inch fish comes from the flowing waters of Thailand such as waterfall streams, indicating that a well-aerated aquarium is especially in order. It is a rather shy species and prefers to remain hidden much of the time, although as with other *Botia* species, its enthusiasm for food brings it forward at feeding time.

An albino (above) and normal (below) specimen of what is probably *Acanthophthalmus robiginosus*. Photos by Dr. Herbert R. Axelrod.

Although *Acanthophthalmus shelfordi* is somewhat variable, as these two photos show, it is usually easily distinguished from the other coolies. Photos by Dr. Herbert R. Axelrod.

The color basically is grayish-tan with a slight green overcast, with usually about ten dark cross bands or vertical bars. These are about as wide as the lighter interspaces between, and there are variable rows of black dots which may be rather irregularly formed on the sides.

The primary difference in this fish and *B. hymenophysa* seems to be in the dorsal fin. The dorsal in *Botia lucasbahi* is either partly or wholly black on the margin, while in *B. hymenophysa* it is clear. According to Smith, *B. lucasbahi* has 9 or 10 branched dorsal rays while the tiger loach has 11 to 13. This may be a subspecies of *B. hymenophysa*.

Feeding as for other loaches. Live foods, especially worms of all types and also blood worms (midge larvae), are especially relished.

BOTIA MACRACANTHA (Bleeker, 1852)
Clown loach

Few freshwater fishes approach the beauty of pattern and coloration of the perennially popular clown loach. This native of Borneo and Sumatra is not easily obtainable even in nature where it is not only less plentiful than some of the less desirable *Botia* but is also only seasonally available. Like other loaches, *Botia macracantha* is a shy bottom-dweller which effectively avoids pursuit by diving into or under roots, debris, etc.

As the name *B. macracantha* would indicate, the preorbital spine is quite sizable in this species (*macracantha* = big spine). It is an effective weapon.

The basic body color is bright orange-red, with three jet-black, wedge-shaped vertical bars on the sides, one of which passes through the eye. Fins are brilliant red, from deep blood red to at times a mercurochrome red.

The clown loach is one of the larger *Botia* species, although aquarium specimens, no matter how pampered, seem unlikely to reach the 12 inch (30 cm.) size reported by

A trio of clown loaches, *Botia macracantha*, probably the most highly desired species of loach and certainly one of the prettiest. Photo by L. Perkins.

On a light-colored background, the horseface loach becomes distinctly lighter and more grayish than its usually tan color. Photo by H. Hansen, Aquarium Berlin.

←——

Common aquarium sharks and loaches. Top to bottom. Left column: *Botia macracantha, Botia hymenophysa, Botia horae, Acanthophthalmus myersi, Acanthophthalmus kuhlii, Epalzeorynchus siamensis, Labeo bicolor.* Right column: *Botia sidthimunki, Botia lohachata, Gyrinocheilus aymonieri, Labeo frenatus, Acanthopsis choirorhynchus, Epalzeorynchus kallopterus, Morulius chrysophekadion.* Photos by B. Kahl.

Weber & de Beaufort in 1916. Improvements in aquarium facilities and maintenance, and especially in feeding, have produced some very large specimens in the past few years, however. Unfortunately, the very large clowns seem to lack the brilliance of their younger brethren.

The color pattern of *Botia macracantha* shows little variation, although adults are less contrastingly marked with black, gold, and red. Photo by M. Chvojka.

Exceptionally large clown loaches of as much as eight inches have been seen in the past few years, but these are almost invariably imported in "giant" sizes. Prices of these leviathanic loaches are usually proportionately outsize.

Properly situated and with aquarium fixtures located in such a way as to lend security without promoting shyness, clown loaches tend more to become rather tame than some of the other *Botia* species. Since secretiveness is their nature, however, they will often show their preference for obscurity if conditions allow.

Catering to the natural preferences of *Botia macracantha*, while creating a less than ideal situation in which the average aquarist can enjoy his fishes and have his visitors share their beauty also, a more "natural" but less observable situation has proved to be a successful spawning vehicle for at least one aquarist. Mr. Werner Nowak of the Montreal Aquarium Society reported that he received six *B. macracantha* from a friend which were between six and seven inches in length. They had been kept in an 80-gallon aquarium where the owner rarely saw them. When he received the fish, two of which were apparently females heavy with eggs, Mr. Nowak placed them in a 35-gallon aquarium containing three large *Echinodorus* sword plants and a great deal of driftwood. The peat-filtered water measured pH 6.2, DH (hardness) 2.0 and nitrite level less than 0.05. A power filter was used and the temperature maintained at 29-30°C. (84-86°F.).

The fish were fed at night before turning the lights off on a mixture of flake food, beef heart, spinach and shrimp pellets. The food was always gone by morning. They did not feed with the lights on.

Discovery of the breeding came when Mr. Nowak needed a sword plant, and upon pulling it up saw a number of small fish scattering. He observed small clown loaches hiding in the roots of the other plants. Seven weeks afterward he had counted 39 baby loaches with an average length of ¾ inch.

Since spawnings of various cobitids are often apparently accidental or perhaps a better word would be incidental, resulting from the fish involved being satisfied with conditions and "doing what comes naturally," this is perhaps the most valid approach to spawning difficult fishes. It has long been a "secret" of Europe's finest breeders to approximate as closely as possible the conditions found in nature for a particular species and letting the fish take over from there.

Although young algae eaters (above) may resemble the horseface loach (below), the differences in mouth and body shape are always enough to distinguish them. Photo above by K. Knaack, that below by R. Zukal.

Top, *Botia sidthimunki*; middle, *Botia macracantha*; bottom, *Botia beauforti*. Photos by B. Kahl.

53

A rather plump, healthy looking *Botia modesta*. The dorsal fin is placed distinctly in front of the ventral fins, but the spot on the tail is larger than usual. In large, healthy specimens like this one the fins are often bright red and the body shiny silver-gray. Photo by H. Hansen, Aquarium Berlin.

BOTIA MODESTA Bleeker, 1865

Although *Botia modesta* is perhaps less striking than its brilliantly colored cousin the clown loach, *B. macracantha* there are several beautiful color variations to this fish which for all practical purposes represent different fish to the aquarist. The body may be varying shades of yellow, blue or green combined with fins which are orange, yellow or red. The ventrals are ordinarily more pale than other fins, and the iris may be yellow, orange or red also. One of the most beautiful and desirable color variations is one in which the smooth-looking body skin is a handsome blue-gray which is difficult to describe, and the fins are a brilliant red-orange.

This is one of the larger loaches, reaching a length in Thailand of close to ten inches. In the aquarium, five inches or over can be considered exceptionally large. Although breeding of *Botia modesta* has not been reported in the aquarium, mature females with fully-developed ovaries have been found in nature which were only 3½ inches in length, indicating that breeding size is certainly reached in captivity.

This is a stocky, heavy-bodied fish which can be aggressive toward other fishes which it considers competi-

The slender-bodied loaches pictured here could just as easily be poorly marked *Botia lecontei* as the more probable *Botia modesta*. The tail spot seems to vary with the mental and physical condition of the fish. In these specimens it is difficult to tell whether the ventral fins are even with or behind the dorsal fin. Photo by M. Chvojka.

Top, *Botia lohachata*; middle, *Botia modesta*; bottom, *Botia hymenophysa*. Photos by B. Kahl.

A nicely colored *Botia beauforti* probing the bottom for food. Photo by K. Paysan.

tive. Plenty of rocks and caves should be available if more than one specimen is present, since they are very territorial. The people of Thailand often apply colorful names to well known fishes, including this one which, according to Smith, is often seen in the markets. *Pla mu*, which means "hog fish," is given to this species because of its large suborbital spines which when erected are similar to the tusks of a hog. Like an Arkansas razorback it can use these "tusks" to slash an enemy. Care is called for in the handling of all larger loaches.

BOTIA SIDTHIMUNKI Klausewitz, 1959
Dwarf loach; Skunk loach

Among *Botia* species, *Botia sidthimunki* is the best all-around aquarium fish of this outstanding group of tropicals. Not only is the coloration striking and beautiful, this is the most diminutive of the *Botia* species discovered so far and the only species which seems to have only good attributes as far as consideration for a community or mixed aquarium of small and medium fishes is concerned.

In its typical color pattern the dwarf loach is not easily confused with any other aquarium species. This is one of the most attractive little loaches and also the smallest. Photo by M. Chvojka.

The darkness of the pattern of *Botia sidthimunki* can vary with the mood of the fish from very dark and heavily banded (above) to extremely light with almost no trace of bands (below). Such variation might also occur between fishes coming from different parts of the range of the species. Photo above by Dr. Herbert R. Axelrod; that below by R. Zukal.

Two juveniles of the Indian loach *Botia dario*. Photo by R. Jonklaas.

With growth *Botia dario* widens and increases the number of stripes
and changes to a more subdued color. Photo by R. Jonklaas.

This active and colorful little loach is quite gregarious and playful and seems much less shy of lighting than its relatives. It also has few of the quarrelsome tendencies sometimes displayed by other *Botia* species. If kept in groups of six or eight, the entire school will often be seen combing over the surface of a rock or other object apparently gleaning algae or other edible substances from its surface.

There is a midside band from the snout to the caudal root, below which the fish is whitish to the belly and above which is black in continuation of the band. Adorning the dark upper surface on each side is a row of prominent gold or yellow blotches which are well defined and are often more or less egg-shaped. The forked caudal is yellowish, with one or two bars or spots on each lobe.

This 1 ½ inch fish from Thailand is easily maintained under conditions described for the genus.

Botia striata is very variable in color pattern and perhaps sometimes sold as a very well patterned *Botia hymenophysa*. However, the head of the two species is very different, the mouth of the zebra loach being under the head at the end of a short snout, while that of the tiger loach is at the tip of the long snout. Photo by G. Senfft.

In the typical pattern the zebra loach has the dark bars arranged in pairs separated by a wide light area. Each dark band is then divided by a narrow light stripe as well. The narrowest light stripes are often absent or broken. Photo by G. Marcuse.

BOTIA STRIATA Rao, 1920
Zebra loach

Botia striata is a handsome fish which appears occasionally in the aquarium trade. The body of this fish from Mysore in southern India is yellowish green, basically, with about nine dark or blackish green vertical bands which alternate with yellow bands. The wide, dark bands become less intense ventrally, and they are medially divided by narrow whitish lines which give quite a distinctive impression. The fins are lightly banded, and the head is banded similarly to the body.

While the pattern is somewhat reminiscent of *B. hymenophysa*, this is a somewhat shorter and stockier fish

The skunk loach, *Botia horae*. Photo by Dr. Herbert R. Axelrod.

When young, *Botia horae* has distinct stripes on the sides, but these are usually lost with growth. Photo by K. Paysan.

Botia hymenophysa, the common tiger loach. Photo by Dr. Herbert R. Axelrod.

A nicely patterned *Botia horae*. In many specimens the skunk stripe is not as distinct. Photo by Dr. Herbert R. Axelrod.

In the most extreme pattern *Botia striata* has the narrow light stripes broken and branched. This is perhaps the most distinctive pattern for the species. Photo by H. Hansen, Aquarium Berlin.

which more closely resembles *B. modesta* in its body shape (not in color).

Care as for other *Botia* species.

Length about 3½-4 inches.

genus *Cobitis*

These are small, compressed and elongate loaches of Europe and Asia. A small, bifid erectile spine which may be more or less concealed is located beneath each eye. Caudal rounded or truncate; air bladder enclosed in a bony capsule without a free portion in the ventral cavity.

Head is compressed and there are six or eight barbels (three or four pairs).

Usually blotched or striped in pattern.

COBITIS TAENIA (Linnaeus, 1758)
Spined loach

Cobitis taenia is found in clear lakes and fast flowing waters in Europe, including eastern England, as well as in Asia and north Africa. For a loach, and a common one, it is a rather demanding fish which must have cool, well-aerated water and a bottom of fine sand.

Because of its habit of picking up mouthfuls of sand, chewing vigorously and expelling the sand from its gill openings it is known as "Steinbeisser" or "stone-biter" in Germany. In nature it feeds on small organisms which it finds in this way and in the aquarium the search continues for small worms and crustaceans, although most foods will be taken.

Cobitis taenia is a very variable species and is not always easy to identify. Usually the line of rectangular spots on the lower side with a row of smaller spots fused to form a solid line on the back is distinctive, but not always. Photo by M. Chvojka.

The reticulated loach, *Botia lohachata*, in two of its patterns. Photo above by Dr. Herbert R. Axelrod, that below by S. Sane.

In this close-up of the head of a clown loach, one can easily see the eight barbels and the groove of the spine below the eye. Photo by Dr. Herbert R. Axelrod.

Spawning sequence of *Cobitis taenia*. The male is much the smaller animal of this breeding pair. Photos by H. Hansen, Aquarium Berlin.

The male nudges the female with his head and feels her with his barbels.

The male twists around the abdomen of the female as a final preliminary to egg laying.

Egg laying occurs during and after a swim by the pair toward the surface of the water.

The eel-shaped embryo and its large yolk are plainly visible in the developing egg.

These two photos leave little doubt as to why the clown loach is the most sought-after loach in the aquarium hobby. Photo above by H. Hansen, Aquarium Berlin, that below by G.J.M. Timmerman.

A beautiful pair of *Botia macracantha*. Photo by Dr. D. Terver, Nancy Aquarium, France.

Like most of its relatives, the spined loach (actually all but *Noemacheilus* are "spined") dislikes bright light and often spends the day retired beneath the sand in some relatively dark place with only the head exposed.

This is a rather handsomely patterned fish. The sides are yellowish or yellow gray and the belly white. There are rows of dark brown spots or blotches on the sides and the upper surface between the dark markings is heavily spotted. There is a stripe from the snout through the eye on each side and the mouth, which is located on the underside, is adorned with three pairs of barbels.

Cobitis taenia is one of the few loaches which has bred in the aquarium under circumstances that have resulted in reasonable patterns. Male adult spined loaches show not only a definite thickening of the second ray of the pectoral fin but also an unusually large scale at the base of the fin which is known as "the Canestrini scale."

Breeding, which occurs in the aquarium only after a cold wintering, takes place in the spring. Breeding occurs at 59-61° F. and the eggs may either be scattered carelessly over the sand or in shallow water among the roots of floating plants or other submerged roots. Babies hatch in 4-10 days depending on temperature and the young are reportedly easy to raise. Feeding is not difficult since most of the nourishment they require is obtained from the mulm on the aquarium bottom.

Cobitis taenia reaches a length of about 4½ inches.

An interesting sidelight was cast on this fish by Gmelin, who was the translator of Linnaeus' *Systemae Naturae* into English, in regard to its natural protection:

> "*The flesh of this fish is hard and tough, so that it is seldom eaten; its prickles are disagreeable, as they tear the hands when touched; but the pike, perch, and water-fowl, will devour them when other food is wanting; so they might be of use to feed those fish in ponds where they are bred.*"

There are several other species of *Cobitis*, including at least two in eastern Europe. This unidentified species probably represents *Cobitis aurata* from the Balkans. Photos by L. Perkins (above) and Dr. Herbert R. Axelrod.

The silvery body and orange fins of *Botia modesta* make up for a lack of flashy patterns in this species. Photo by Dr. Herbert R. Axelrod.

All sharks and loaches require hiding places. Rock or ceramic tunnels like this one are especially useful as they allow the fish to be seen even when hiding. Photo by Dr. Herbert R. Axelrod.

With proper feeding and a tank which makes them feel secure, these *Botia lecontei* will soon look as shining as the *Botia modesta* on the opposite page. Photo by K. Knaack.

To a fish already equipped with a switch-blade knife, what could give more added protection than to be disagreeable to the palate?

In Burma Dr. Herbert R. Axelrod photographed this specimen of a small loach known as *Lepidocephalichthys berdmorei*. The resemblance to *Cobitis*, especially the eastern European species, is striking.

genus *Lepidocephalus*

These are typical loaches of the Far East which are found for the most part in swift brooks and streams with sand or gravel bottoms, although they are also found in lakes and swamps in which the bottom may be covered with mud or silt. There are six or eight barbels, and there is a bifid or two-pronged spine below the eye. The dorsal is located far back.

These are among the burrowing loaches and when frightened they often disappear rapidly into the bottom soil. They seem to dig into sand or gravel substrates quite easily, using the spiny first ray of the pectorals to help dig themselves in.

In nature they feed primarily on bottom dwelling insect larvae, worms and crustaceans which can be rooted out.

LEPIDOCEPHALUS GUNTEA (Hamilton, 1822)

Lepidocephalus guntea (sometimes misspelled *guntae*) is found throughout most of India and has been occasionally imported.

The body color is usually yellowish to greyish, or as Day puts it, "dirty yellowish," with a light stripe or band extending from the center of the snout to the base of the tail, where it terminates in a black ocellus or a deep black blotch just above midway. Above and below are a series of dark blotches, and the dorsal and caudal show numerous rows of dark spots. The underside is pale.

The dorsal begins midway between the eye and the caudal base; no lateral line is present. The suborbital bones are scaled and there is also a band of scales from the eye to above the opercle (*Lepidocephalus* = scaled head). As with many loaches there is a large two-pronged suborbital spine which can be erected and locked in place as a

Two variations of the little *Botia sidthimunki*, the normal pattern below and an unusual striped variant above. Photo above by M.F. Roberts, that below by Dr. Herbert R. Axelrod.

Botia striata is one of the rarer aquarium loaches. Photo by H. Hansen, Aquarium Berlin.

This little Burmese loach has been identified as *Lepidocephalichthys berdmorei*, but little is known about it. Photo by Dr. Herbert R. Axelrod.

defense mechanism.

Length up to about 6 inches (15 cm).

LEPIDOCEPHALUS THERMALIS
(Cuvier & Valenciennes, 1846)

Ranging in southern India, the Malabar coast and Sri Lanka, *L. thermalis* is rather similar in appearance to *Cobitis taenia*.

The body is greyish or grey-green to sandy-colored, with irregular blotches along the lateral line and on the back, giving a rather marbled effect. Usually there is a black spot on the upper caudal base. Caudal with five or six "V" shaped brown stripes in Ceylonese specimens, others sometimes with four bands. Five rows of spots on dorsal, outer rays of pectoral spotted.

It is of interest that the type specimen was collected from a hot spring, resulting in the specific name *"thermalis"* being chosen. It is said to prefer quiet pools with loose silt and sediment to flowing waters. In parts of Sri Lanka (Ceylon) during the dry season it is the last cyprinid to survive in puddles which are littered with the corpses of other fishes, often still wriggling through the mud when little else is left.

According to Deraniyagala this fish is essentially a vegetarian but has a definite fondness for mosquito larvae.

genus *Misgurnus*

This genus is comprised of rather eel-like and usually dull-colored bottom-living loaches of Europe and Asia. Anteriorly the long body is cylindrical in shape, becoming laterally compressed or flattened from the sides toward the posterior. There are ten barbels (five pairs).

MISGURNUS ANGUILLICAUDATUS (Cantor, 1842)
Dojo; Japanese weatherfish

The Japanese weatherfish, or Dojo as it is sometimes called, is found through northeast Asia into central China, Japan and somewhat southward. It is quite similar in appearance and habits to the European weatherfish, *M. fossilis*.

Like the other weatherfish, the Dojo prefers a mulmy or muddy bottom in which it can burrow, often leaving only the head above the turf. The *Misgurnus* species are rapid and evasive swimmers. Combined with their ability to dive out of sight beneath the sand, their quickness and agility make removal from a planted and decorated aquarium a difficult and sometimes frustrating experience.

The Japanese weatherfish goes through many different color varieties depending on the locality at which it is taken. The heavily spotted fish shown here seems to be one formerly known as *Misgurnus mohoity*. Photo by H. Hansen, Aquarium Berlin.

Lepidocephalus jonklaasi, a loach restricted to the island of Ceylon. It was named in honor of Rodney Jonklaas, the famous collector of tropical fishes. Photo by Dr. Herbert R. Axelrod.

A non-descript loach of the genus *Noemacheilus*. Without knowing where this specimen was collected, it is almost impossible to identify it. Photo by K. Paysan.

Ceylon is the home of many attractive loaches. This is *Noemacheilus botia*. Photo by Dr. Herbert R. Axelrod.

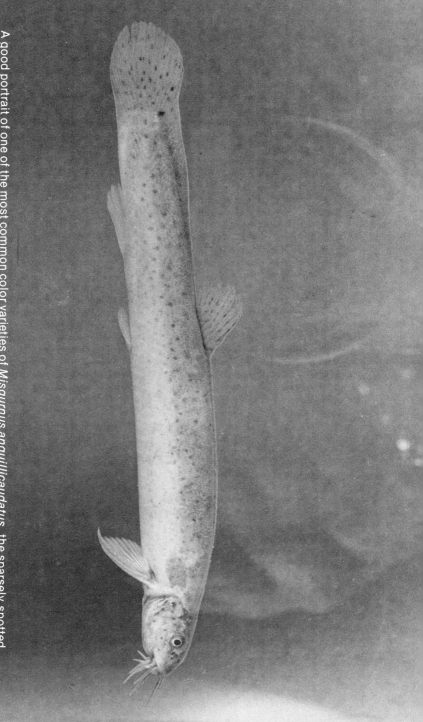

A good portrait of one of the most common color varieties of *Misgurnus anguillicaudatus*, the sparsely spotted form once called *Misgurnus mizolepis*.

A closeup of the anterior part of the body and head of *Misgurnus anguillicaudatus*, showing the barbels, embedded scales, and the long pectoral fin spine. In many loaches the long pectoral spine indicates the fish is a male. Photos by Dr. Herbert R. Axelrod.

Noemacheilus fasciatus, a pair above and a female below. Photo above by Dr. Herbert R. Axelrod, that below by H. Hansen, Aquarium Berlin.

The black spot in the dorsal fin and the black line at the caudal fin base identify this little Ceylonese loach as *Noemacheilus notostigma*. Photo by Dr. Herbert R. Axelrod.

Temperature and water conditions seem to make little difference to *Misgurnus,* and these loaches appear to be equally at home in either tropical or coldwater aquaria, or in the outdoor pond.

Since weatherfish of this genus are more obviously whiskered than most loaches, they are often confused with catfishes.

MISGURNUS FOSSILIS (Linnaeus, 1758)
Weatherfish

The famous "weatherfish" of eastern and central Europe is so named for its sensitivity to changes in atmospheric pressure, and reacts to a falling barometer with rather

The weatherfish is one of the more commonly seen "unusual" loaches in the pet shop. The striped color pattern usually is distinctive and more-or-less constant. Photo by R. Zukal.

nervous activity, "paceing" up and down the aquarium glass. They were for a time reportedly kept in bowls and aquaria in Europe literally to serve as "living barometers" because of their supposed ability to predict an impending storm. This sensitivity is generally thought to be detected through the gas bladder, the Weberian ossicles and the inner ear, although there is some thought that the fish may instead be reacting to other circumstances ordinarily accompanying barometric changes.

This is one of the rather eel-like loaches which is fond of burrowing in the substrate. At times only the head is visible above the sand with its standard set of five pairs of short, stiff barbels, while at other times the fish may be totally submerged.

This is one of the hardiest fishes imaginable. Its intestinal respiration system is remarkably efficient and water quality seems to concern it very little. In nature it lives in slow moving, standing and even stagnant waters in which other fishes might often perish, and even if the water dries up it can dive into the muddy bottom and estivate until it rains or the water returns.

The body is long and cylindrical with rather ocher-colored sides. The upper side is brownish to dark brown and the underside yellow to orange. There is a dark longitudinal band on the side accompanied sometimes by others which are less prominent. The sides are also at times variously spotted. Dorsal and caudal usually dark and often spotted.

This fish has been known to spawn in outdoor ponds with mud bottoms. Males are said to have larger pectoral fins which are squared, with the second ray thickened. Females are heavier-bodied with rounded pectorals which are smaller.

The weatherfish is a bottom feeder which accepts almost any fish food. It has considerable capacity and its form plus its burrowing ability allow it to reach food which

Several of the African *Labeo* species have very high dorsal fins in the adult. This is *Labeo altivelis*, a juvenile specimen above and an adult below. Photos by Dr. E. Balon.

The two species of *Epalzeorynchus, kallopterus* above and *siamensis* below, are *Labeo*-like fishes from Southeast Asia. They are commonly sold as sharks whenever imported. Photos by Dr. Herbert R. Axelrod.

A spawning sequence of the weatherfish. This species follows the usual loach pattern of the male feeling and nudging the female and then twisting his elongate body about hers. Both fish then rapidly move to the surface.

At the surface the egg laying begins and may be continued on the bottom. The relatively large eggs are shown attached to a sprig of *Myriophyllum*. Photos by K. Knaack.

The striking contrast between the red tail and black body help make *Labeo bicolor* the most popular shark. Photo by R. Zukal.

Since its first introduction to the hobby, the Chinese algae eater,
Gyrinocheilus aymonieri, has been a standard fish in almost all
fresh-water community tanks. Photos by Dr. Herbert R. Axelrod.

Sometimes species of *Garra*, a cyprinid, are imported and sold
along with algae eaters. Photo by Dr. Herbert R. Axelrod.

other fishes could not, qualifying it as an excellent scavenger.

Weatherfish are good jumpers and should be kept in covered aquaria.

This species sometimes reaches a length of one foot.

genus *Noemacheilus*

Noemacheilus is a genus of small loaches ranging in Europe, Asia and into northern Africa. They are found mostly in clear, cool, swift hill streams and mountain streams with gravel or sand bottoms. Even in places where they are extremely abundant, with even the quietest and most stealthy approach the stream may appear barren to the observer because of the nocturnal nature of these fishes.

There are numerous species in southeast Asia, a few of which are occasionally imported for the aquarium. Despite the fact that most are only a few inches long, according to Hugh M. Smith the mountain people of Thailand are quite fond of them as food and go to considerable lengths in their capture, "fishing" for them in places which would appear to outsiders to be totally unproductive. A small stream is dammed with stones, mud, leaves, twigs, and branches so that it is diverted either into an old bed or into a new channel prepared for the purpose. In the old bed the gravel and sand are scooped out using coconut shells, the hands, etc. and an amazing number of fish are uncovered, including other loaches as well as *Noemacheilus*.

Noemacheilus species should generally be kept in relatively cool, well-aerated water. Their aquarium should be moderately planted and the bottom should be of smooth, large-grained sand or gravel.

Like some of the cichlids, some loaches are infamous for rearranging the aquarium by spitting out sand and gravel. *Noemacheilus kuiperi*, shown here, has such a habit. This species is similar to the more familiar *N. fasciatus* but differs in the number of dorsal rays and other details. Photo by Dr. W. Wickler.

These young red-tailed black sharks still show the black shoulder spot and the white tip on the dorsal fin. Photo by H. Hansen, Aquarium Berlin.

An extremely high-finned African shark, *Labeo congoro*. Photo by Dr. E. Balon.

Labeo bicolor. Photo by the author.

Noemacheilus species can be distinguished from other loaches by the absence of the suborbital or preorbital spine which most loaches use as a "switch-blade knife."

NOEMACHEILUS BARBATULUS (Linnaeus, 1758)
Stone loach; Groundling

Noemacheilus barbatulus is widespread throughout Europe and its subspecies range through northern and central Asia into Siberia.

They have three pairs of barbels, with one pair longer than the other two. The body is rather long and fairly slender; the mouth is small and downward directed. The upper lip is extensible. Color is basically golden to olive brown and the sides are blotched darker as well as spotted in a quite variable manner. The dorsal is located about mid-way on the back and is spotted, as are the caudal and pectorals. The rows of dots sometimes form bars.

This is *not* a tropical fish and the water must be clear, well-aerated and not over about 68°F. in temperature.

The European stone loach, *Noemacheilus barbatulus*, is a dully colored species preferring colder waters. It is seldom offered for sale. Photo by L. Perkins.

The early spawning behavior of the stone loach follows the usual pattern of nudging, feeling, and body twisting. The relatively stout body does not permit as definite a body twisting as in *Cobitis* and *Misgurnus*. Photos by L. Perkins.

A small specimen of the rainbow shark, *Labeo erythrurus*. Photo by Dr. Herbert R. Axelrod.

The smaller specimen of *Labeo cylindraeus* shows the obvious derivation of the scientific name. Photo by Dr. E. Balon.

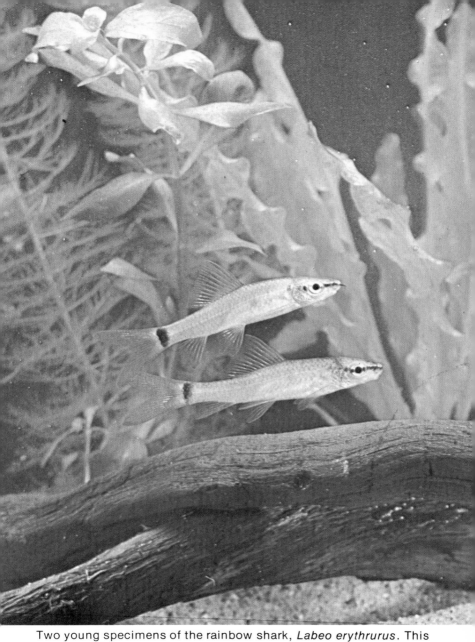

Two young specimens of the rainbow shark, *Labeo erythrurus*. This is a generally smaller and more slender species than the red-tailed black shark. Photo by K. Knaack.

With the beginning of parallel swimming (top photo), it is obvious that the mating behavior is coming to a climax. The pair swims to the top and begins to lay their large eggs. These eventually become attached to submerged plants. Photos by L. Perkins.

Most accounts indicate a distinct preference for live food but some authors credit the stone loach with being omnivorous and quite unchoosy about its fare. The aquarium should be moderately planted with sturdy plants, since this is a vigorous burrower. A pebbly bottom with stones is recommended. Hiding places should be available under rocks and stones.

Breeding occurs in April and May, when eggs are deposited on stones and pebbles and also among the plants. Eggs reportedly hatch in about a week and the babies are rather large, about the size of baby guppies. Growth is rapid.

Sexes are not easy to distinguish except during the spawning season when the female is obviously thicker in girth. Males, however, are said to have slightly more intense coloration and can also be distinguished by the larger pectoral fins, which are thickened on the second ray and display horny papillae on the inner margin. Pectorals of females are rounded, the second ray is not thickened and the papillae are lacking.

A xanthic or yellow form occurs in nature upon occasion. In this color variation the body and fins are yellow to orange and the eyes are black.

NOEMACHEILUS BOTIA (Hamilton, 1822)

Noemacheilus botia, from northwest India to Assam, has been occasionally seen in the aquarium and seems in some ways more typical of the qualities which aquarists have come to associate with loaches than some of the other *Noemacheilus* species.

Reaching a length of about 4¾ inches, *N. botia* is a bit heavier-bodied than most of the *Noemacheilus* species and the profile seems more *Botia*-like. The three pairs of barbels are distinctly visible. The body color is greyish green on the sides with dark blotches. Belly is light to whitish. Dorsal and caudal are spotted.

Labeo lineatus, an interestingly patterned shark.
Photo by Dr. Herbert R. Axelrod.

Labeo erythrurus. Photo by the author.

Although its color pattern lacks most of the flashy black and red of some of its more popular relatives, the slim lines and shiny silver and gold of *Labeo forskalii* make it a popular species. Photo by R. Zukal.

Noemacheilus botia, an attractive little species from southern Asia. Notice that the caudal fin is nearly rounded, not forked as in *N. fasciatus*. Photo by H. Hansen, Aquarium Berlin.

This is one of the less demanding *Noemacheilus* species which, like more familiar aquarium cobitids, will accept almost any food. It also feeds on algae or algae substitutes.

Water should be relatively cool and well aerated as well as clear.

There are no reports of breeding or of sex distinctions.

NOEMACHEILUS FASCIATUS
(Cuvier & Valenciennes, 1846)
Barred loach

The coloration and pattern of this fish from the Greater Sunda Islands including Java, Sumatra and Borneo is reminescent of some of the patterns found among

The barred loach, *Noemacheilus fasciatus*. Above, a pair, the heavily egg-laden female sitting on the bottom. Below, the male barred loach has a deeply forked tail fin with the upper lobe long and pointed. Photos by Dr. Herbert R. Axelrod.

Although attractive in body shape and the high fins, the color pattern of this *Labeo lunatus* from Africa leaves something to be desired. Photo by Dr. E. Balon.

Labeo frenatus. Photo by the author.

The red-finned shark, *Labeo frenatus*. This supposed species is very close to the rainbow shark, *Labeo erythrurus*, in color and shape, and it is very doubtful if the two can be separated in the aquarium. Photo by R. Zukal.

the coolie loaches, *Acanthophthalmus*. The body is adorned with eleven to twenty brown vertical bands interspaced with yellowish lines. The belly is yellowish or whitish and the fins delicate yellow. There is a dark band at the root of the tail and usually another through the eye, which is rather small. Some specimens have a spot on the dorsal.

N. fasciatus is another of the relatively few *Noemacheilus* species in which mature males bear a fleshy preorbital hook. Males of the closely related species from North Borneo, *N. olivaceous*, bear small tubercles on the membrane between the first two branched pectoral rays. This is true also of *N. fasciatus*, although the patch of tubercles is wider and covers the entire membrane between the rays.

As with other *Noemacheilus* species, small live foods including worms and insect larvae such as mosquito larvae and blood worms (larvae of gnats of the family Tendipididae) are preferred, along with frozen brine shrimp, etc. This is, however, an easily fed, omnivorous fish which will accept and thrive on most fish foods. A hardy, undemanding fish, although it may become quite territorial and even aggressive.

Reaches about 3½ inches in length.

NOEMACHEILUS MASYAE Smith, 1933
Arrow loach

One of the most attractive loaches of the genus *Noemacheilus* is the arrow loach, *Noemacheilus masyae* from Thailand. According to Hugh M. Smith it is one of the most widely distributed of the *Noemacheilus* species in Thailand, and because of its distinctive form and pattern it could easily become quite popular if its availability to aquarists was increased through more frequent imports.

This is a rather small species, usually 2½-3 inches, with a slender body, long barbels, and a deeply forked caudal or tail fin of which the upper lobe is much longer. Both lobes are pointed. The body is usually olive brown with a series of 14-20 dark brown saddle-shaped spots on the back which extend downward toward the lateral line. Along the lateral line are the same number of corresponding brown spots, with a small, jet-black spot surrounded by a pale yellow area just at the base of the caudal fin. Another black spot is found at the lower anterior part of the dorsal fin.

Males are distinguished by the possession of a cartilaginous hook extending backward from the preorbital. This corresponds to the preorbital spine found in most loaches, but lacking in *Noemacheilus* species.

Despite being from what is usually considered a "tropical" area, the arrow loach, as with others of its genus, prefers water which is not too hot. Well-aerated water in the lower 70's is necessary to keep them at their best. This species is more free-swimming than most.

The many species of *Noemacheilus* found in southern Asia all look about the same to the aquarist, only a few standing out in the crowd. This little *Noemacheilus* is not *N. fasciatus* because it does not have the deeply forked tail fin, but that is about all one can say for it. Photo by H. Hansen, Aquarium Berlin.

There are numerous species of *Labeo* which are seldom seen in the aquarium, although they do have attractive colors and shapes. These species simply cannot compete with the more popular and colorful *Labeo bicolor, Labeo frenatus*, and others. Photo above of *Labeo nasus*; photo below of *Labeo parvulus* by Dr. Herbert R. Axelrod.

The blotchy color pattern of the young *Labeo variegatus* is distinctively different from that of any other common aquarium shark. Photo by Alimenta-Brussels.

Labeo variegatus. Photo by the author.

genus *Gyrinocheilus*

GYRINOCHEILUS AYMONIERI (Tirant, 1883)
Sucking "loach"; "Chinese" algae eater

This is a remarkable fish which seems to have a proclivity toward receiving inappropriate names. Known generally in America as "Chinese algae eater," it is not native to China but instead to Thailand and Cambodia. In England it is called the "sucking loach," in spite of not being a loach. It is only this misnomer which has found this hill-stream fish a place in this book.

G. aymonieri is perhaps the most efficient eater of algae available to aquarists. Not only does it scrape, rasp and glean the green pest from the rocks, walls and plants in the aquarium, it does so with a minimum of detriment to the more desirable aquarium horticulture.

The Chinese algae eater actually belongs to its own family and not to the loaches. The color pattern varies greatly with age, but apparently only one species, *Gyrinocheilus aymonieri*, is imported. Photo by R. Zukal.

Look closely and you can see the separate opening at the upper edge of the operculum through which water is drawn into the gills without the use of the mouth. This is an adaptation to allow the sucking mouth to hold the fish on the bottom even in very swift streams. Photo by M. Chvojka.

Promoting the efficiency of the fish's ability to move over the aquarium on an algae-removal mission is the fact that breathing is accomplished entirely through the gill openings, which contain both inhalant and exhalant openings. This leaves the mouth free for either grazing or hanging on, which is often necessary in the swift streams in which these fish are often found in nature.

The Siamese algae eater, as it might be more appropriately called, reaches a length of about six inches in the aquarium, and sometimes becomes rather aggressive. Maturity occurs at about five inches, and although spawnings have occurred they are infrequent. Reports indicate that spawning takes place in a depression or furrow which is excavated by the adults. Parental care is apparently exercised in a manner similar to that of *Labeo frenatus*.

Omnivorous and long-lived, this interesting fish easily earns its keep.

Labiobarbus, possibly *burmanicus,* a species of shark often mistaken for the somewhat similar *Osteochilus hasselti.* Photo by Dr. Herbert R. Axelrod.

The Bala shark, *Balantiocheilos melanopterus*, has an unmistakable pattern of silver body and black and white fins. Photo by Dr. Herbert R. Axelrod.

If it were more commonly imported, there is little doubt that the beautiful colors of *Labiobarbus festiva* would make it one of the more popular aquarium sharks. Photo by A. Norman.

An adult *Labeo variegatus*. Photo by the author.

SHARKS

Sharks for the aquarium are for the most part rather bold and pompous creatures, at least individually. Those which prefer retiring to the background usually do so in order to avoid the physical abuse of another more dominant fish, usually the same species. They are mostly active and curious, often mischievous creatures whose main goal in life often seems to be to simply live every minute of it.

AQUARIUM FURNISHINGS

Most sharks need and appreciate plenty of swimming room. While some of the smaller *Labeo* species do reasonably well in smaller aquariums, fifteen gallons or up should be considered minimum for any but a temporary housing arrangement. In a twenty-five or more they will show their appreciation for the increased spaciousness by greatly increased growth rate and improved, more intense color. The really large species such as *Morulius* require very large aquariums.

If several of a species are kept together, provide them with plenty of retreat in the form of rocks, roots and sturdy aquarium plants. *Sagittaria* species are excellent background plants for the sharks such as *Labeo* and *Osteochilus* which continually graze and nibble their way over the aquarium furnishings, since the leaves of these plants are less delicate than some and at the same time are attractive and functional.

Caves and overhangs can be provided in accordance with the territorial nature of some species, as well as providing additional retreat areas for those which might need them.

Medium or medium-coarse sand can be used, small enough to be picked up or at least easily pushed about in the cleaning efforts of the fish.

WATER CONDITIONS

Most of the aquarium fishes known as sharks are hardy creatures which can thrive under most aquarium conditions. Those which are most familiarly known as sharks, the members of the genera *Morulius* and *Labeo*, are almost ideal in this respect and will survive many aquarium disasters during which those fishes with less tenacity of life succumb. Others such as *Osteochilus* and *Labiobarbus* are almost equally tenacious and with reasonable care all of these will live for years. There are some, such as *Balantiocheilos*, which are perhaps a bit less rugged but nevertheless capable of great longevity.

Water conditions seem to have little effect on their well-being as long as extremes in pH and hardness are avoided. It's almost tempting to say that if the water is not strong enough to either dissolve boot leather or pickle it, and if a two-pound rock will sink in it, there is probably a shark somewhere that will live in it. More seriously, a pH range of 6.6-7.4 is acceptable to all, with most showing no particular discomfort even a bit beyond this range. Concerning hardness, medium hard or softer water seems perfectly acceptable, although "zero soft" water could possibly be improved by bringing the hardness level up to 1 or 2 DH. DH as considered here is rated as grains per gallon which also equals 17.9 ppm (parts per million) hardness content. Hardness is, of course, a reference to the content

There are few more impressive aquarium fishes than a large, well developed black shark. Photo by K. Paysan.

Osteochilus spilopleura, a species seldom seen in the aquarium. Photo by A. Norman.

The black shark, *Morulius chrysophekadion.* Photo by the author.

of calcium and magnesium salts in the water, the presence of which affects the ability of soap to form suds and also the general health and breeding ability of some fishes.

Generally speaking, most local water supplies are suitable for most sharks. Very young fish are more sensitive than older ones, and if they have been kept in water drastically different from your own, they should be acclimated over a few days.

For breeding attempts, relatively softer water is recommended, with pH around neutral.

Temperature range is wide for most species, which seem quite comfortable between 65-85° F. At the higher temperatures, water should be well aerated.

As with other fishes, partial water changes made periodically invigorate the fishes and improve their color in most cases. Aged water, or at least completely dechlorinated water, is a must, since cyprinids and their near relatives are among the most susceptible fishes to chlorine poisoning.

FEEDING SHARKS

Unlike their notorious marauding namesakes whose insatiable appetites have prompted their gastronomical inventories to harbor such goodies as tin cans, wooden boxes, a rubber raincoat, various pieces of the human anatomy including a tatooed forearm and even a bulldog with a rope still tied around his neck, aquarium sharks are satisfied with simple fare. Most, such as *Labeo* and *Morulius*, are cyprinids which are omnivorous to an extent and will accept almost any food offered them.

Labeo and *Morulius* and their near relatives which are known as "fringe-lipped fishes" are for the most part nibblers and grazers, continually moving over the surfaces of plant leaves, rocks, aquarium glasses and the floor of the aquarium, gleaning from them algae and any other nourishment which might be found. Since algae is a natural constituent in the diet of many of these fishes, good lighting is desirable since it helps promote the growth of algae. An excellent substitute for algae is an occasional alfalfa rabbit food pellet or two or cooked spinach, either fresh or canned. For very young or small fish, strained baby spinach is very good. Almost all will accept and benefit from boiled oatmeal or rolled oats which can be cooked up in sizable batches and refrigerated until it is used completely. Don't overdo the quantity, since it gets a bit "yeasty" after a few days. This can be avoided by freezing into small blocks or balls adequate for one feeding and thawing them as needed.

While the oatmeal is being prepared it can be mixed with other ingredients either to increase its "appeal" or to increase its nutritional value. Two favorites which are often added while the oatmeal is cooking are ground beef heart and ground dried shrimp. The beef heart should be finely ground and is best not "cooked" into the oatmeal but simply mixed while the oatmeal is still hot. Since the bulk of the diet of most fishes such as *Labeo* is essentially vegetation in one form or another, as indicated by the extremely long, coiled intestine, oatmeal in itself is an excellent staple since it is high in nutritional value. It has the added advantage of being one of the few soft foods which hardly clouds the water at all. During feeding it "hangs together" very well, releasing very few small particles, and its softness allows larger fishes to take large pieces and smaller ones to bite off or suck off more suitable portions. Digestion is amazingly complete and there is relatively little waste even from large fishes.

Few foods produce better growth in fishes in general than regular feedings of beef heart. Even those aquarium sharks which are mostly vegetarian in nature show great enthusiasm for beef heart (or ox heart as it is known in

Pangasius sutchi, the only catfish commonly called a shark. Photo by Dr. Herbert R. Axelrod.

The Apollo shark, *Luciosoma spilopleura*. Photo by the author.

England), and whether it is fed separately or combined with oatmeal or other fare, it is an excellent conditioner. It should be finely ground or scraped from a frozen strip which accomplishes the same thing in making the food swallowable for the relatively small and toothless mouths of these fishes.

BREEDING CONDITIONS

The aquarium sharks which have so far been successfully spawned in captivity are small species of *Labeo* from Thailand. While this has by no means been a regular occurrence, there seem to be patterns which could possibly be used as guidelines in future attempts with similar species.

A large aquarium seems in order because of the often aggressive nature of these fishes. Water should be reasonably soft, less than 100 ppm or about 4 DH, and neutral to slightly acid according to some of the successful reports. Rocks and caves should be provided since these are sometimes used as spawning sites. Water should be well aerated at a temperature of about 82° F.

If possible, potential breeders should be separately conditioned on live food or other high quality foods and vegetation, preferably algae, until the female(s) can be distinguished by an obvious plumpness. When in top condition, a large, colorful male can be placed in the breeding aquarium with one or two ripe females.

Breeding is further discussed under some of the individual species.

SPECIES OF "SHARKS"

With few exceptions the fishes which in the aquarium hobby are known as "sharks" are actually members of the family Cyprinidae, commonly known as carps or minnows. The majority belong to the genus *Labeo* and similar fishes which have large, sometimes shark-like dorsal fins and forked caudals. *Labeo, Morulius* and several others belong to a group known as "fringe-lipped fishes" since their often oversized, extensible lips are fringed with folds of rough skin which enables them to rasp algae and other substances from the surfaces of plants, stones, etc. as well as simply ingesting other food substances in a more conventional fashion. As with other cyprinids there are no teeth in the jaws, necessitating the roughly textured and powerful lips for gleaning purposes.

Morulius chrysophekadion, the original and perhaps most shark-like of aquarium "sharks," seems more deserving of the name than *Luciosoma*, which seems hardly shark-like by any stretch of the imagination.

There are other "sharks" including catfishes or Siluriformes, and because of the fascination of the name, others will appear from time to time on the market. Some will be more shark-like than others, and better names could be coined in many instances. There is little doubt, however, that the borrowed label has helped popularize and keep available some of our most fascinating aquarium fishes.

genus *Labeo*

Labeo species are generally moderately long-bodied and cylindrical in shape, with a rather rounded snout. The mouth is inferior, meaning the upper jaw is much longer than the lower, and the lips are thickened, with one or both having an inner fold with a rather horny covering which forms a sharp inner edge. The dorsal is often tall and sail-like, especially in larger fish.

These are mostly hardy and long-lived fishes, several of which make magnificent show fish in very large aquaria. Most are somewhat aggressive against those of the same or similar species, or against any fish considered competitive. Very large specimens often have a tendency toward mellowing in disposition.

The most familiar *Labeo* spp. for the aquarium come generally from Thailand and nearby areas, with a few from Africa. India, however, has a number of species also, some of which would make quite handsome aquarium fishes if they were regularly imported. Some of these grow to extremely large sizes, at least one, *L. gonius,*exceeding five feet according to Day.

It is of interest that during the British occupation of India those frustrated sons of Izaak Walton who were uprooted by military or foreign service from their native land of trout and salmon streams and relegated to a country where the water was warm and the fishes mostly carps, often found certain satisfaction in fishing for *Labeo* species. They found them to be not only strong but also wary . . . in addition, they were excellent eating in most cases, although they were rather bony.

Illustrating the omnivorous nature of the *Labeo* appetite is the following from THE ROD IN INDIA by H.S. Thomas (1881):

> "*Bait with paste or dough such as you fancy. . . The natives scent their paste with the most offensive, untouchable, unmentionable matters. I daresay asafoetida would answer the same purpose; I have not tried.*"

LABEO BICOLOR Smith, 1931
Red-tailed black shark

The red-tailed black shark, or simply red-tailed shark as it is sometimes called, is one of the most beautiful and spectacular of freshwater aquarium fishes. At its best, which is its normal condition with reasonable care, this native of Thailand is one of those few fishes which is immediately striking even to those uninterested in fishes, yet still intriguing and challenging to the connoisseur, the collector and the experienced breeder of many years.

With clean, clear water which avoids extremes in pH and is not unreasonably hard, combined with good feeding, body color is seldom less than a deep, almost void-like velvety black. At times a black shoulder spot shows

The shade of the black body color varies a great deal in the red-tailed black shark. In specimens which are cold, upset, or poorly fed the body becomes more grayish than black and it is possible to easily see the black shoulder spot. Photo by R. Zukal.

through the body blackness about midway between the opercular edge and the beginning of the dorsal fin. The jet-black dorsal is sail-like in a manner reminiscent of a shark, while the anal and ventrals or pelvics are also deep black. Pectoral fins are clear. In contrast to the inkiness of the forward makeup of the fish is its crowning glory, the strikingly brilliant and deeply forked tail or caudal fin, which is Mercurochrome-red to velvet red. Except that the dorsal occasionally has an enamel-white tip, there is only black and red (*bicolor* = two color).

When more than one red-tailed shark is housed in a community aquarium, apparently unmerciful bullying can occur unless sufficient cover is provided in which the underdog or underdogs can hide. With sufficient cover, the only harm which usually results is one fish far outgrowing the other or others because of its dominance. While several small fish will sometimes abide with reasonable harmony together, peck-orders are evident and usually unchanging in fish permanently kept together, although even a brief removal and replacement of a fish can result in a "personality change" which can land it higher or lower in the scheme of dominance. I have had this occur simply by removing a *Labeo* long enough to be photographed and returning it to the original aquarium.

Labeo bicolor is occasionally bred in the aquarium and is probably less difficult than might be imagined. As is often the case with many fishes which are considered difficult, the primary factor seems to be conditioning. Because of the competitive nature and territorialism of red-tailed sharks and their close relatives, it is best to distribute potential breeders in several aquariums. In this way the growth rate is more likely to be about even than when one dominant fish rules the roost and hogs the food. Maturity is more likely to be reached at near the same time if the fish were near the same age and size to begin with providing that conditions are approximately equal in the different aquariums. Equally important is that in the case of red-tailed sharks and their near relations, absence makes the heart grow, if not fonder, at least more receptive.

While red-tailed black sharks are sometimes imported in ridiculously small sizes which reflect comparatively low prices, specimens an inch or more long are recommended for purchase since they are hardier. Beginning with small fish, a year of good feeding and roomy conditions will bring them easily to breeding size, which in nature is three inches or more. Males often grow faster than females and are noticeably slimmer, although well conditioned males have a satisfying plumpness about them also.

The breeding aquarium should be about fifteen or twenty gallons and should be well provided with rocks and caves since spawning usually occurs on the underside of a ledge, in a cave or on a rock. Although they have success-fully spawned in water with a pH of 7.8 and hardness of more than 300 ppm (parts per million) or about 18 DH, water which is near neutral (pH 7.0) and less than 100 ppm seems more reasonable and has scored a number of successes within the group.

Aside from a few notable exceptions such as the American creek chub and fallfish (*Semotilus atromacula-tus* and *S. corporalis*) there are relatively few cyprinids that exhibit interest in their eggs other than as caviar. *Labeo bicolor*, however, is a less prolific spawner than most cy-prinids or carps, producing an average of perhaps 30-60 eggs in a spawning in a preselected, reasonably defensible place. The female or females are usually chased away by the male, who continues to fan the eggs and keep them clean by "mouthing" them until they hatch. Sometimes the male is also removed and an air stone placed near the eggs to aerate them. At about 80° F. hatching takes approxi-mately two or three days and in two or three more days the fry are free swimming, having absorbed their yolk-sacs. If the male is left to care for the eggs, he can be removed at

Fully developed young specimens of *Labeo bicolor* are truly two-colored, black and red, except for a touch of shiny white at the tip of the dorsal fin. Even this last touch of white will be lost with further growth, however. Photo by M. Chvojka.

any point after the eggs hatch, which is perhaps safer than leaving him present.

As with other egglayer fry, feeding should begin only after they are free swimming. First food can consist of infusoria, commercially available fry foods such as the liquid food available in tubes, or egg yolk infusion prepared by the aquarist. My own preference for most egglayer fry too small to immediately eat newly hatched brine shrimp is to use green water as a first food, turned that color from exposure to the sun, with resultant growth of small plants in large numbers. In a few days the youngsters are ready to have brine shrimp added to their diet. Micro-worms are also very good at this point.

Young fish grow reasonably fast and in six or eight weeks they may be one-half inch in length, at which time they are still rather silvery gray. The dorsal at this point begins to blacken, followed by the body. In a few weeks coloration, including the red tail, is complete. Fully colored young fish have a white tip on the dorsal.

LABEO ERYTHRURUS Fowler, 1937
Rainbow shark

Of the *Labeo* species native to Thailand and surrounding areas, as far as beauty of coloration is concerned *Labeo erythrurus* is second only to *L. bicolor*, the red-tailed black shark. *Labeo erythrurus,* commonly known as the rainbow shark, is quite similar in appearance to its more common congener, *Labeo frenatus*, the red-finned shark, but the colors of the rainbow shark are much more intense. So great is the similarity that H.M. Smith suggested the possibility that *L. frenatus* might simply be the young of *L. erythrurus*. In *Labeo erythrurus* the origin of the dorsal is well in advance of the ventrals or pelvics, while it is midway between the tip of the snout and the middle of the caudal peduncle or tail root, directly over the beginning of the ventrals in *L. frenatus*.

The body color of *Labeo erythrurus* ranges from olive green, as in *L. frenatus*, to a highly intense blue-black or charcoal. Dorsal, anal and caudal are intensely red or mercurochrome-red in healthy and mature fish. Combined with the blue-black or charcoal of some specimens the effect is most striking and few tropicals are more beautiful than this particular variation in full bloom. There is a dark band from the snout to the eye and a large black spot entirely across the caudal peduncle, both of which are obscured in dark specimens. The anal is edged in black.

Unfortunately, as with other close relatives, this is a rather quarrelsome fish with its own kind. When more than one rainbow shark is present definite dominance patterns are established. If only two are present it may eventually be necessary to separate them unless plenty of refuge is available. Several fish are more likely to achieve a workable hierarchy than only two.

This species tolerates a wide variety of water conditions with apparently little effect, although reasonably soft

Labeo erythrurus. The two red-finned sharks are badly confused, and it is not at all certain if there are one or two species. Both *L. frenatus* and *L. erythrurus* were named by the ichthyologist Fowler, who had a reputation for "creating" new species where none actually exist. Photo by Dr. Herbert R. Axelrod.

water on the acid side seems to intensify color. Temperatures between 70-80° F. are best, although 5° lower or higher do no apparent harm.

Almost all foods are acceptable, although vegetation should be included in the form of algae, alfalfa pellets or spinach.

This is a long-lived species which may reach five inches.

LABEO FORSKALII Ruppel, 1835

Labeo forskalii is found in the Nile Basin and tributaries of the Blue Nile. This is one of the largest of aquarium sharks, reaching 18 inches or more in nature.

Young fish are a rather "fish green" or greyish green, shading toward silver below. Larger fish are olive green above, shading lighter, sometimes yellowish, below. Scales on flanks of larger fish have pinkish centers. The snout is rounded and fleshy in appearance, rather swollen looking. There is a curved groove across the upper surface of the snout. Barbels are minute and under folds of skin.

This is a hardy and long-lived fish which should be kept in a large aquarium with fishes of similar size capable of taking care of themselves. *Labeo forskalii* is very aggressive against its own kind and is best kept only one to an aquarium. It is not usually aggressive toward other fishes unless they are considered competitive.

L. forskalii is omnivorous and will accept almost any food. Brine shrimp, beef heart, cooked oatmeal, pellet and tablet foods are eaten with relish. Vegetation such as cooked spinach or alfalfa pellets should be fed occasionally.

LABEO FRENATUS Fowler, 1934
Red-finned shark

The red-finned shark, *Labeo frenatus*, is native to

northern Thailand and is one of the more frequently imported *Labeo* species.

The body color is olive grey to dark olive. There is a dark band from the tip of the snout through the eye to the gill cover. There is a black band on the caudal or tail root and the fins are bright red, almost blood red in fish in top condition. This fish is very similar to *Labeo erythrurus*, from which according to Smith it differs in placement of the dorsal fin. In *L. erythrurus* the front of the dorsal fin is inserted anterior to the ventrals, while in *L. frenatus* the dorsal is inserted directly over the insertion of the ventrals.

As with other *Labeo* species, this is a somewhat aggressive fish, especially with its own kind or other similar fishes which it deems competitive. Most of this aggression is relatively harmless, although during breeding there are reports of other fishes having been killed and even stripped of their fins.

Successful spawning has occured in water which is slightly acid and moderately soft. Parents excavated a nest at one end of the aquarium and eggs were deposited on the glass bottom. Parental care was displayed, cleansing and guarding the eggs and helpless fry.

This is a hardy, long-lived fish which thrives under a wide range of conditions. An omnivorous feeder which, like other fringe-lipped fishes, should have vegetation in its diet.

Length is about 3½ inches.

Sexes are distinguished in well-conditioned fish by the fuller, more robust body of the females. This plumpness is easily seen from above or below. Mature males have a black border on the anal fin.

LABEO MUNENSIS Smith, 1934

White-tailed shark

While importations, if any, have been few, *Labeo munensis* from eastern Thailand promises to be equally outstanding with the *Labeo* species which have already become so firmly entrenched in the aquarium. Recorded by Hugh M. Smith in 1934, *L. munensis* has a reddish brown body with a large black dorsal, anal and ventral or pelvic fins. These black fins are all distinctively bordered with a well-defined white edge. The tail is white.

The fish is apparently not rare since it is said to be familiar to local Thai fishermen who call it *pla soi lord*, which means "tubular school fish."

Care and conditions should be similar to requirements of *L. bicolor* and *L. frenatus*.

LABEO VARIEGATUS Pellegrin, 1901
Harlequin shark

Labeo variegatus from the upper Congo is, especially at maturity, the most beautiful and handsome of the African *Labeo* species. Young fish are yellowish mottled with brown, black and some red. In adults, the dorsal is concave and sail-like, carried with a disposition indicating the bold and vivacious nature of the fish. The body is dark brown above, yellowish gray below. The sides are dark brown-gold or brown and each scale is with a crimson spot. Fins and sides are reddish, gold and brown which mingle strikingly in changing light.

This is a hardy but unfortunately rather aggressive fish which should be kept with other fishes capable of defending themselves. Aggression is often directed toward an individual fish which the shark considers competitive, often a large cichlid. A large, brightly illuminated aquarium with heavy planting, good hiding places and good aeration is best. Water conditions are uncritical, and a temperature of 70-80° F. is fine.

This is a heavier feeder than the more familiar Asian species. Rather omnivorously gluttonous, it consumes large quantities of live, frozen and flake foods as well as

This young harlequin shark, *Labeo variegatus*, has a long way to grow before it is mature, but it has already begun to get the high, sail-finned dorsal of the adults. Notice also the very large tail fin. Photo by G.J.M. Timmerman.

oatmeal, spinach and alfalfa pellets. Breeding has not been reported.

The colors and form of this beautiful show fish improve with age, which can be a number of years in the aquarium if good conditions and plenty of space are supplied.

This was one of the outstanding fishes first made available to the American aquarium hobby during the so-called "Congo Bonanza" of the mid 1950's. This was a historic period for the aquarium hobby since for the first time large scale importations of African fishes, most of which had not been seen by fishkeepers, were coming into the country. Since that time only the inconsistency of availability has kept the harlequin shark from becoming among the most popular of *Labeo* species.

Labeo variegatus is hardy, handsome and long-lived. It makes a superb show fish.

LABEO WEEKSI Boulenger, 1909

Labeo weeksi is found in the middle and upper Congo and was another of the fishes which was among the large importations which occured in the mid 1950's. It still shows up occasionally.

Labeo weeksi is more attractive than some of the other *Labeo* species which sometimes find their way into aquaria from the Dark Continent. The dorsal is tall and falciform, with the anterior part (last unbranched and first branched ray) greatly prolonged into a handsome and striking appendage. Fins are rather greenish to reddish brown, and the body is yellowish or yellow-green with brown longitudinal lines running between the series of scales. Scales are dark-edged, forming a somewhat net-like pattern. Barbels may be partly obscured by folds of skin.

As with most African *Labeo* species, *L. weeksi*, which reaches 10 inches or more in nature, is omnivorous and will accept all foods with gusto. As with the others its at least partially vegetarian nature should be considered.

Typically rather quarrelsome.

genus *Labiobarbus*

These are relatively large, barb-like fishes from Burma through the Malay Archipelago. They are notable for their very long-based dorsal fin, which has caused at least one species to be called "shark."

LABIOBARBUS SP.
Striped Labiobarbus

Several *Labiobarbus* species are quite similar in description, including the handsome striped species illustrated. The body is silver, with several longitudinal rows of dots following rows of scales and comprising the striped pattern. Dorsal bright pink and concave, with striking

No, the bottom fish is not *Osteochilus hasselti*, but *Labiobarbus burmanicus*. The two are commonly confused but are really easy to separate by looking at the dorsal fin—*Osteochilus* has less than twenty rays, *Labiobarbus* almost thirty. Photo by G. Marcuse.

black edge; extremely long-based. Caudal is deeply forked, pink to red, with a black line on each lobe; outer rays light.

The upper lip is fringed; there are two pair of barbels.

Care as for other similar fishes such as *Osteochilus*. Omnivorous, very hardy. A handsome, mild-mannered species which was obtained as "Dangila barb." The generic name *Dangila* was at one time applied to some of the species.

Reaches as much as eight or ten inches.

The juvenile *Morulius* has light fin edges, that of the caudal fin being very broad. Notice the white tip of the dorsal fin like that of the red-tailed black shark. The head appears to be made up mostly of eyes. Photo by Dr. Herbert R. Axelrod.

genus *Morulius*

Morulius is very similar to *Labeo*, and as far as the aquarist is concerned, should be treated the same. This is the original "black shark" and is one of the larger aquarium fishes.

MORULIUS CHRYSOPHEKADION (Bleeker, 1850)
Black shark

Widespread through Thailand and surrounding areas, this was the first aquarium "shark" to be imported. Named obviously for its shark-like appearance, the coal-black coloration found in healthy young fish is immediately striking and the fish has been popular since first introduced many years ago.

Black sharks are extremely hardy and will grow to a large size in a large aquarium. I have personally had fish reach more than 14 inches. With age the color changes considerably from velvet black to an increasingly lighter bronze gray. Each scale has a yellowish or reddish spot in the center. While most water conditions seem completely suitable, frequent partial water changes intensify the black in even larger and older fishes.

This is a handsome, most impressive show fish for the large aquarium even after some of the intensity of its blackness has faded since the replacement coloration is equally attractive in its way. The aggressive nature of *M. chrysophekadion* seems to mellow considerably with increasing age and size.

With growth the fish darkens, losing most of the white fin edges, and the eye becomes relatively smaller. The white caudal fin is the last to turn black. Photo by G.J.M. Timmerman.

A heavy, omnivorous feeder which grows rapidly with good feeding and plenty of room. Good algae cleaner.

Morulius chrysophekadion was known for a time as *Labeo chrysophekadeon*. As a matter of fact, the genera *Labeo* and *Morulius* are extremely similar. In *Morulius* the lower lip is entirely separated from the isthmus, which is the projection reaching between the opercular openings or at the "throat" of the fish, by a deep groove. In *Labeo* the lower lip is joined to the isthmus by a bridge.

As with certain other cyprinids the black shark at maturity and upon sexual ripening displays "pearl organs" or little wart-like breeding tubercles on the snout, top and sides of the head. H.M. Smith observed these on very young fish which were only 2-4 inches in length as they left the swamp where they had been hatched in that same year.

The Thai have colorful and often descriptive names for many of their fishes, and the black shark is known to them as *pla ka* or *crow fish* because of its black color. In Cambodia is it known as *trey kaek*, which also means crow fish, not only because of its blackness but its ability to utter a raucous croak.

genus *Osteochilus*

This genus of East Indian fishes belongs to the group of Old World minnows with inferior or underslung mouths and fringed sucking lips which are known as fringelips or fringe-lipped fishes. They are similar in some ways to *Labeo* and at least one species has been sold as a "shark."

It is of interest that the sucking response in some of these fishes is strongly dependent on contact or touch stimulus to the fringed, fleshy lips, and that fishermen in southeast Asia often bite the lips off these fish before placing them in holding pens with other fish. This is to keep the other fishes from being damaged in the crowded condi-

A beautiful, and truly black, black shark. This fine specimen has lost all light fin edges and is a uniform sooty black. With further growth the black will change to bronzey and the fish loses some of its attractiveness. Photo by J.L. Martin.

tions by contact from their bodies stimulating the sucking response in the fringelips.

OSTEOCHILUS HASSELTI
(Cuvier & Valenciennes, 1842)
Silver shark

Osteochilus hasselti, sometimes sold in the trade as the silver shark, is widely distributed through Thailand and the Malay Archipelago. The name *Osteochilus* means bony lip in reference to the hard, bony prominence of the lower jaw, which actually projects over the lower lip. As with its near relatives belonging to the genus *Labeo*, the lips are fringed and protrusible, equipping the fish for

Osteochilus vittatus, a common Southeast Asian shark, is sometimes imported. The relatively short dorsal fin identifies it as an *Osteochilus*. The black stripe tends to fade and break with growth. Photo by Dr. Herbert R. Axelrod.

Closeup of *Osteochilus vittatus*. The barbels are very short compared to most *Labeo* species. Photo by Dr. Herbert R. Axelrod.

continually grazing over rocks, plants, aquarium walls and floor in a search for algae and other food items. The body is greenish above, whitish on the belly and the sides are rather cream-colored with six to eight dark lateral bars.

Young specimens show a dark spot at the caudal base which fades with age. As the fish ages, the long-based, almost sail-like dorsal turns yellowish to reddish and the caudal, ventrals and anal become increasingly reddish.

This is an active, relatively peaceful fish for its size which reaches over a foot in length in nature and perhaps eight or ten inches in a large aquarium. Mock battles oc-

Two *Cyclocheilichthys apogon* (top and middle) and a silver shark, *Osteochilus hasselti* (bottom). Although similar at first glance, the dorsal fins show that these are really very different fishes. *Cyclocheilichthys* has an especially heavy and barbed spine at the front of the dorsal fin. Photo by Dr. Herbert R. Axelrod.

cur with its own and similar species, or those it considers competitive. Little harm is done.

As with other *Osteochilus* species or "bony-lipped barbs" as they are known in the United Kingdom, the silver shark is highly esteemed as a food fish in Thailand and other countries where it is found.

This is an easily cared-for, long-lived and magnificent show fish for a mixed aquarium of larger fishes.

genus Balantiocheilos

These are slender, streamlined fishes of the family Cyprinidae, better known as carps or minnows. A peculiarity of the genus is the horseshoe-shaped mouth, with a pocket or purse-like compartment behind the lower lip (*Balantiocheilos* = purse-lip).

BALANTIOCHEILOS MELANOPTERUS
(Bleeker, 1851)
Tricolor or Bala shark

The tricolor shark or Bala shark, *Balantiocheilos melanopterus*, is an outstanding fish although it is one of the least shark-like of the aquarium "sharks." In Thailand it is known as *pla hang mai* which means burnt-tail fish.

The tricolor shark has a long, silvery and streamlined body with a powerful forked tail or caudal fin. The dorsal is fairly large, and, like the anal and caudal, is from orange-yellow to red-orange in color. Dorsal, anal and caudal are all strikingly outlined in black.

This fish is less omnivorous than *Labeo* species and is more demanding about the quality of its food. While most frozen and freeze dried foods are accepted, live foods are preferred. Most specimens will accept high quality flake foods with enthusiasm also, although occasional individuals are reluctant. The mouth is rather small, and in spite

151

The young Bala shark is much more slender than adult or half-grown specimens, and the fins are not as sharp-ly edged in black. Photo by Dr. Herbert R. Axelrod.

With growth, the body becomes deeper and the black on the fin edges becomes more sharply defined. The fish above is about half grown. In the adult the body is very deep compared to the juvenile on the facing page and the black fin pigment is heavy and sharp-edged. Photos by M. Chvojka (above) and G.J.M. Timmerman (below).

of the oral capacity of its namesake, proper food size is a consideration.

Healthy and well fed tricolor sharks can become rather large in the aquarium, although they are unlikely to reach the ten inch size which is attained in nature. They are rather peaceful in comparison to some of the other sharks and make outstanding show fish in a community aquarium of medium and larger fishes as long as the latter are not aggressive. As size increases the colors of the fish seem to lose some of their intensity.

Water seems not to be critical as long as extremes are avoided in pH and hardness. Temperature should be reasonably warm, preferably at least 75° F. Lower temperatures will be tolerated but color and activity are better at 75-82° F.

Spawning is not reported.

genus Luciosoma

The genus *Luciosoma* is found in the East Indies and is perhaps the least shark-like of the aquarium fishes which have borne that title. These are long, slender fishes with large mouths, and are decidedly more pike-like than shark-like.

They are the largest members of the subfamily Rasborinae found in Thailand, reaching a length of 10-12 inches, which is large enough to give them some economic importance as a food product.

LUCIOSOMA SPILOPLEURA Bleeker, 1855
Apollo shark

The popular application of the name "shark" for aquarium cyprinids seems to have been stretched to its imaginary limits in the case of the so-called Apollo shark, *Luciosoma spilopleura*. Any connection between this southeast Asian fish and the Greek god Apollo seems equally obscure. It is, however, an interesting and rather outstanding fish and the trade name has served the purpose of helping a worthwhile fish become established.

Native to Borneo, Sumatra and Thailand, this swift and streamlined minnow frequents the upper layers of water where in nature it feeds on insects and other small surface creatures. The mouth, which is adorned by a rather long pair of maxillary barbels, is deceptively large and the fish cannot be trusted with fishes smaller than itself.

This is a handsome fish which in proper lighting displays iridescent blues and greens just above a striking dark longitudinal band which actually is composed of blackish brown spots extending from the head to the caudal base. The caudal or tail is forked and each lobe has a dark band edged in light. Both pectorals and ventrals are longer than in most similar fishes and the anterior rays of the ventrals are further elongated into filaments.

Luciosoma is aggressive with its own kind and with other active surface fishes. In nature a length of nearly one foot is recorded, although aquarium specimens are likely to remain smaller. Spawning has not been reported.

Feeding is not difficult. High quality flake foods are acceptable as well as other foods which float or sink slowly. *Drosophila* and small meal worms are excellent and are eaten with great enthusiasm.

Water quality and temperature are not critical as long as extremes are avoided. The aquarium should be roomy and provided with both planting and open areas if more than one Apollo shark is present, so that potential refuge is available to the underdog or underdogs if needed. It is very important that the aquarium be covered at all times possible since *Luciosoma* species are tremendously efficient jumpers.

genus *Pangasius*

The catfishes of this genus belong to the family Schilbeidae of Asia and Africa. It is the most numerous genus of catfishes from Thailand where many aquarium fishes originate, and two members are among the world's largest catfishes. At least one species is regularly imported and is often commonly referred to as a "shark."

PANGASIUS SUTCHI Fowler, 1937
Iridescent shark, Siamese shark, smoky glass catfish

Pangasius sutchi is one of the few aquarium catfishes to have been dubbed with the title of "shark." Actually, if appearance is any criterion, it is more deserving than some. It is swift and streamlined and has a rather shark-like profile with its forked tail and rather prominent dorsal fin.

The young iridescent shark is an attractive fish with the black stripes on the sides heavy and separated by a narrow silver area. In some ways it is more attractive than the larger specimens but not nearly so active or impressive in the aquarium. Photo by R. Zukal.

In half-grown *Pangasius sutchi* the stripes on the sides begin to grow diffuse and will eventually fade to a dusky on silvery. The shape of the head and the relative sizes of the eyes and barbels also change. Photo by G. Marcuse.

The Siamese shark is an outstanding fish in a number of respects. It is among the relatively few free swimming and diurnal catfishes, and its handsome form and coloration combined with its almost ceaseless activity compliment any aquarium in which the size of the fish and its actions are compatible. The eyes are extremely large and arresting. There is a broad dark band from the head to the caudal base with a lower dark band from the head to just above the anal, with these bands and the dark dorsal surface separated from each other by silvery-white interspaces. The dorsal is gray-black, as are the ventrals and pectorals. The caudal is also dark with whitish edges. The belly is whitish and the anal white with a dark median band. The overall appearance gives an impression of glassy steel-blue or steel-gray patterning which flows perfectly with the form and movements of the creature.

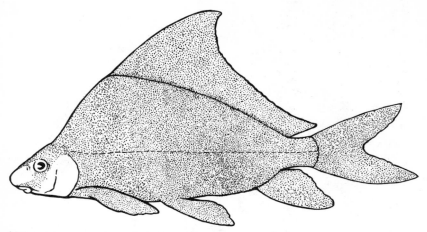

Although a member of the sucker family and not the cyprinids, the Chinese *Myxocyprinus asiaticus* could easily be called a shark because of its high dorsal fin.

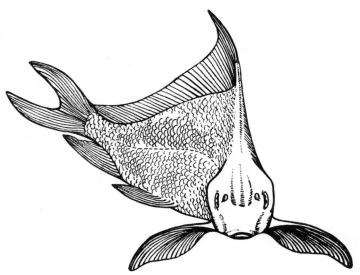

    P. sutchi is by nature a schooling or shoaling fish. To be at its best it should be kept in groups of several fish. Kept singly, the fish often becomes sluggish and inactive. *Pangasius sutchi* is a member of the family Schilbei-

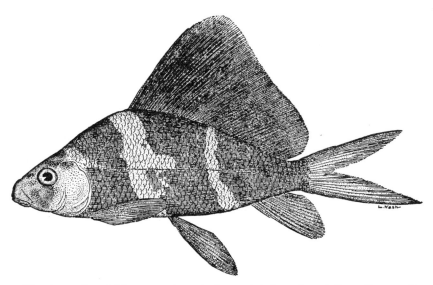

The juvenile of *Myxocyprinus* is less plainly colored than the adult and still has the very high dorsal fin.

dae to which belongs one of the world's largest freshwater fishes, *Pangasianodon gigas* of the Mekong River. Oddly, this huge creature, which reaches over nine feet in length, is a toothless vegetarian. Because of the often glass-like appearance of the schilbeid catfishes they are among those known as "glass catfishes."

Feeding the Siamese shark is not difficult since it is omnivorous. Pellet food is particularly appreciated, along with flake food, brine shrimp, beef heart, etc. Vegetation should also be offered such as spinach (cooked) or alfalfa rabbit food pellets. Boiled oatmeal is also good.

Water conditions are not critical if extremes in hardness and pH are avoided. Temperature range should be 70-82° F., with good aeration provided especially at the upper end of this range. *Pangasius sutchi* is capable of taking atmospheric air at the surface if the need arises.

This is an excellent fish for the community aquarium of medium and larger fishes of its own size. It seldom reaches over six inches in the aquarium.

INDEX

Page numbers in **bold** indicate illustrations